Winning Against the Enemy

Marilyn Hickey

Winning Against the Enemy

practical steps for
SPIRITUAL WARFARE

Marilyn & Sarah
MARILYN HICKEY MINISTRIES

Winning Against the Enemy

Copyright © 2024 by Marilyn Hickey Ministries

All rights reserved. No part of this publication may be reproduced, distributed, or transmitted in any form or by any means, including photocopying, recording, or other electronic or mechanical methods, without the prior written permission of the publisher, except in the case of brief quotations embodied in critical reviews and certain other noncommercial uses permitted by copyright law.

Marilyn Hickey Ministries
PO Box 6598
Englewood, CO 80155-6598
marilynandsarah.org

ISBN 978-1-938696-41-1

Unless otherwise indicated, Scriptures are taken from the New King James Version®. Copyright © 1982 by Thomas Nelson. Used by permission. All rights reserved.

Scripture quotations marked (AMPC) are taken from the Amplified® Bible,
Copyright © 1954, 1958, 1962, 1964, 1965, 1987 by The Lockman Foundation. Used by permission. lockman.org

Scripture quotations marked (ESV) are taken from The Holy Bible, English Standard Version® (ESV®), Copyright © 2001 by Crossway, a publishing ministry of Good News Publishers. All rights reserved.

Scripture quotations marked (NASB) are taken from the (NASB®) New American Standard Bible®, Copyright © 1960, 1971, 1977, 1995, 2020 by The Lockman Foundation. Used by permission.
All rights reserved. lockman.org

Scripture quotations marked (MEV) are taken from The Holy Bible, Modern English Version
Copyright © 2014 by Military Bible Association. All rights reserved.

Scripture quotations marked (NIV) are taken from the Holy Bible, New International Version®, NIV®. Copyright © 1973, 1978, 1984, 2011 by Biblica, Inc.™ Used by permission of Zondervan. All rights reserved worldwide. www.zondervan.com The "NIV" and "New International Version" are trademarks registered in the United States Patent and Trademark Office by Biblica, Inc.™

Scripture quotations marked (TLB) are taken from *The Living Bible*, Copyright © 1971 by Tyndale House Foundation. Used by permission of Tyndale House Publishers, Carol Stream, Illinois 60188.
All rights reserved.

Assembled and Produced for Marilyn Hickey Ministries by
Breakfast for Seven
breakfastforseven.com

Printed in the United States of America.

Contents

Introduction	vii
1 Winning Through Deliverance	1
Strategies for Winning	26
2 Winning Against the Devil	37
Strategies for Winning	60
3 Winning Through Resurrection Power	89
Strategies for Winning	105
4 Winning Against the Antichrist	113
Strategies for Winning	175
End Notes	187
About Marilyn	190
Receive Jesus Christ as Lord and Savior	193
Learn more about Marilyn & Sarah Ministries	195

Introduction

Do you tend to think that God only does miracles in the lives of certain people — evangelists, pastors, or those who are "super spiritual?" Maybe you think that God only does the supernatural in certain places — like churches or revival tents. Or that He only moves in particular countries or nations far away from where you live.

But that's just not true. God has given **every believer** the power to win through the miraculous **every day** and **everywhere.**

I have experienced a lifetime of walking in the supernatural. I have experienced healing and deliverance in my own life, but I have also seen the lives of countless others radically changed through the power of God. I have also faced obstacles that seemed hopeless and failures that seemed like they were too much. But I have stood in faith during situations in which it looked impossible to win, and God gave me the victory!

He has that same victory for you today.

Maybe you're facing circumstances that are threatening to destroy your faith. Perhaps you or a loved one have an addiction or spiritual battle that looks all but lost. I believe that God wants to encourage you and strengthen your spirit today.

This book is a selection of teachings on how to win against the enemy. You will learn how to be delivered in your circumstances, how to win against the devil, how to use the resurrection power of Jesus, and how to recognize the Antichrist and his spirit of deception.

Although spiritual warfare can seem like a precarious topic, I think you will find this book to be both practical and uplifting. Each section is filled with biblical teaching and real-life examples. At the end of each section, you will be given step-by-step strategies to use every day as you begin to walk the victorious and miraculous path that Jesus has for you.

INTRODUCTION

My prayer is that, through this book, you will discover how to win against the spiritual attacks that come against you and that you may learn to be *"confident of this very thing, that He who has begun a good work in you will complete it until the day of Jesus Christ"* (Philippians 1:6, emphasis added).

It's not over until you win!

1

Winning Through Deliverance

You may not like the circumstances you are in. It may be in relation to your health, finances, work, or some other area of life. Maybe you find yourself in a place that is unpleasant, and you don't want to face it each day. The Bible tells how you can change your circumstances for the better.

Purpose in Your Heart

Let's look at the circumstances of four young men in the Old Testament. First of all, we'll see just how bad their circumstances were. They were taken captive to Babylon, so to begin with, they were slaves. They had left all community affiliations and influence. They had left their loved ones, and their parents were probably killed. When they arrived in Babylon, they found they would not have a normal physical life, for they were made eunuchs. This was a very dark situation!

On top of all that, their names were changed from Daniel, Hananiah, Mishael, and Azariah to Belteshazzar, Shadrach, Meshach, and Abednego. *Ah* at the end of a name means that it comes from Jehovah, which means "self-existent or eternal." *El* means strength, might, or power — Elohim comes from this word. So Hananiah and Azariah are derivatives of Jehovah; Mishael and Daniel are derivatives of Elohim.

Let's look at the meanings of these names. Hananiah means "Jehovah has favored," and Shadrach, the Babylonian name given to him, means "command of Aku." Aku was the Babylonian god of the moon. Azariah means "Jehovah has helped," and he was given the name of Abednego, which means "servant of Nebo." Nebo was the Babylonian god of wisdom. This was the name of one of their idols. Mishael, which means "who is what God is," was changed to Meshach. There is confusion around what Meshach means; "that draws with force," "guest of a king," or "the shadow of the prince" are a few different potential meanings. Daniel means "judge of God." His name was changed to Belteshazzar, which means "favored by Bel." Bel was the favorite idol of Nebuchadnezzar, the king of Babylon (Daniel 4:8).

Why were their names changed? To transform their natures. Not only did the Babylonians change their environment and alter them physically, but they also did their best to change their natures. They didn't want the young men to have spiritual names because it would call to mind the God whom they loved and served. The Babylonians wanted to get their attention away from their God and put it on idols.

Here these young men are, in the darkest situation they could be in, with the Babylonians changing everything in their lives they could possibly alter — even trying to get them to change their God. But light is greater than darkness, and no matter how difficult the situation may be that you are in, if you will do what these men did, circumstances will not change you. You will change circumstances. If you don't change circumstances in your life, they will change you. There is nothing in between.

Sometimes we say, "I'm not going to be black or white; I'm going to stand in the middle. I don't have to be a bold witness and talk about Jesus. I don't have to be a sinner and act like a sinner. I'll just be in the middle of the road." If you get in the middle of the road, you'll get run down and shattered because you can't stay there. Either you are for God and going His way in life, or you are in darkness. You won't read anything about twilight in the Bible. It is either light or darkness.

I believe that Christians should have a spiritual desire to change their circumstances. The first step is to do what Daniel and his friends did; it was the beginning of changing their circumstances. *"But Daniel purposed in his heart . . ."* (Daniel 1:8). They purposed in their hearts that they would not be changed by circumstances and would continue to serve God.

You never make a decision without getting the opportunity to express what you purposed in your heart. Have you ever said, "That's the way I will be; that's the way I will be," and found an opportunity the next day to show the way you will be?

The Bible tells us that right away, God did something very special for Daniel and his friends. Changing circumstances involves more than your own effort. You purpose in your heart; then God begins to do the supernatural, but not until you first purpose in your heart.

God brought Daniel and the three Jewish children into tender, loving favor with the head of the eunuchs. That is a move of God. When you purpose in your heart, He will begin to line things up for you.

God gave them favor and love in the eyes of this Babylonian man. Why should a Babylonian love a group of Jews? They are trash as far as he is concerned — just slaves — but God gave them favor. Did you know that God can give you favor with unsaved people? You do not have to compromise to have favor! Have you ever heard someone say, "If you'll be like everyone else, they'll really like you." That's a lie of the devil! If you'll be like God, they'll like you better. If you purpose in your heart, they will like you better.

When I was in St. Louis one time, a pastor related an interesting story to me. Hilton Sutton was scheduled to appear at his church for a prophecy series. Many of the congregation worked for Jewish people, and they decided it was their "fishing" time. There had been some very strong antisemitic feelings that they wanted to pull down, so they asked God for favor with the Jewish community. The people began to invite Jewish merchants to come hear Hilton Sutton, and 50 or 60 Jewish people came to the meeting. God so touched their hearts that the congregation had favor with these merchants, who gave them a 40-percent discount when they shopped in their stores. They don't even give that to others in the Jewish communities!

Purpose in your heart, and God will move upon people and give you favor. The very thing you want will be yours. You'll have favor with people that will astound those around you.

When Daniel and his friends purposed in their hearts, they said, "We cannot eat the food you are serving the other men in training." I don't know what was wrong with the food. It could have been that it was pork, and the Jewish dietary laws would not permit them to eat pork. It could have been that the alcoholic beverages were part of their decision — that they would not drink wine or be drunks just to fit in with the crowd.

There is a lot of alcohol in our junior and senior high schools today. Students need to purpose in their hearts that they don't have to be an alcoholic to be popular. After making that decision, they need to make it public when they're offered a drink. Be bold and say, "I don't drink because I am a Christian."

These young men said, "We don't want to eat the food, but we don't want to get the chief eunuch in trouble. We like him; he's our friend. Just feed us the food we feel we should have for 10 days, and if we don't look healthier than the others, then deal with us according to what you see" (Daniel 1:8–14, author's paraphrase).

So they ate pulse, a mixture of vegetables and lentils; at the end of 10 days, they looked healthier than those eating the other diet. Notice, they purposed in their hearts, they began to act on their faith, they had loving favor with the head of the eunuchs, and then they had better health!

Did you know that following Jesus will give you better health? You'll be physically stronger when you purpose in your heart to serve Him. Who wants to lose his brains and blow them out with drugs? Who wants to ruin his liver by the time he is 27? These are things that happen, but if you will purpose in your heart, you will have a healthier body.

The Rewards of Faithfulness

After all this, God did something more for these young Jewish men. He gave them knowledge and understanding of dreams, and they were 10 times wiser than anyone the king knew. I believe God can make you 10 times wiser than the other students when you purpose in your heart. God can make you 10 times better on your job than anyone else. Why not? I think we should always claim we are the best, because when we purpose in our hearts to serve Him, He will put us over supernaturally. You may say, "I'm not that smart, Marilyn." I don't think they were that smart either. I think God made them that smart.

In the second chapter of Daniel, Nebuchadnezzar had a dream that was so unique and unusual that when he woke up, he was deeply troubled over its content.

It used to bother me that I didn't have more spiritual dreams. My dreams were usually so silly they hardly meant anything. I knew they weren't anything spiritual, so one day I said, "Lord, why don't I have spiritual dreams? I read the Scriptures before I go to sleep, and I'm usually memorizing verses. I still don't have spiritual dreams." Then the Lord told me something as I studied this story of Nebuchadnezzar, and it is found in the book of Job.

"For God may speak in one way, or in another,
Yet man does not perceive it.
In a dream, in a vision of the night,
When deep sleep falls upon men,
While slumbering on their beds,
Then He opens the ears of men,
And seals their instruction." (Job 33:14–16)

Why did He speak to them in dreams? Because they didn't listen to Him when they were awake. That encouraged me.

Nebuchadnezzar wouldn't listen while he was awake, but God could get to him at night. You will notice that God used this method many times to speak to heathen kings. They wouldn't listen to Him through His prophets, so He spoke to them in dreams and got their attention. So if you are not having a lot of spiritual dreams, maybe it is because God can get your attention without a dream.

When Nebuchadnezzar couldn't remember his dream, he called in his wise men and said, "Tell me my dream! Quick! Tell me my dream!"

They said, "Tell your dream? You're asking something we cannot do. Tell us your dream and we will give the interpretation, but we can't tell you the dream."

"No, no, no!" he said. "I've been feeding and clothing you and educating you and have spent a great deal of money on you. You should be able to tell me my dream."

They said, "We can't do that."

So Nebuchadnezzar decided to kill all the wise men. The news came to Daniel, and he said, "Wait! Tell him not to kill us yet. We're going to have an all-night prayer meeting." In that prayer meeting, God showed Daniel the dream.

Look at their spiritual behavior. It pays to pray. Because they purposed in their hearts, made a decision not to compromise, confessed that God is real, and acted on their decision, they became healthier, they had favor, they were smarter, and God gave Daniel the king's dream.

Then Daniel told Nebuchadnezzar his dream and the interpretation of it. Now let's watch what happened with Daniel. Nebuchadnezzar made a very strong statement after Daniel revealed his dream and the interpretation. He was really amazed. *"The king answered Daniel, and said, 'Truly your God is the God of gods, the Lord of kings, and a revealer of secrets, since you could reveal this secret'"* (Daniel 2:47).

Nebuchadnezzar had a revelation of the Trinity, and he was not in the Kingdom yet. He said, "He's the God of gods (that's the Father); He's Lord of kings (Jesus is the King of kings); and a revealer of secrets (the Holy Spirit)." Daniel and his friends were not only changing their circumstances, but they were about to change a king. *"Daniel petitioned the king, and he set Shadrach, Meshach, and Abed-Nego over the affairs of the province of Babylon; but Daniel sat in the gate of the king"* (Daniel 2:49).

See what happens when you purpose in your heart to serve God and to not compromise? God will make you the head and not the tail. These three Jewish boys were placed in positions a lot of Babylonians would have loved to have, and they were just slaves! God can make leaders out of slaves who are devoted to Him.

Notice that Daniel sat at the gate of the king. That means he was one of the elders of the city who made all the major judicial decisions. He was one of the kings' number-one men. You say, "But Marilyn, he was a young eunuch and a Jewish slave!" Yes, but he was devoted to God, and he purposed in his heart. God will put you over others when you do that.

Facing Tests and Trials

Now they were in very high positions, and you can be sure the devil was about to test their positions. I will not pretend to you that it will be easy to live a life that does not compromise with the devil — one that makes a bold stand and says, "This is where I will stand, and that settles it." The devil will do his best to push you out of that stand.

In Daniel 3, Nebuchadnezzar, who was an ungodly man, set up a big idol out on the plain. In one place in this chapter, it says he made the idol himself, but I doubt he did it alone because it was so big. It was about nine feet wide by 90 feet tall, and it was made of gold. Of course, Babylon was the wealthiest country in the world at that time.

That was not the only idol Nebuchadnezzar served, but he put it up and said, "I want all the leaders of all the nations I have conquered to come at a certain season and bow down to this tall idol when I play the musical instruments." Why did he do this? He had a lot of idols. The nations he had conquered had a lot of idols, too. He was trying to have a one-world religion.

The king said, "It is all right if you have these other idols, but once a year you must come to Babylon and worship this one golden idol on the plain of Dura. And just in case there are any rebels in the crowd, I want you to know that if you do not bow down, I have a furnace into which we will throw you." That might have taken care of the rebels, but Shadrach, Meshach, and Abednego did something in the first chapter of Daniel that is important: they purposed in their hearts. It is important for you to purpose in your heart. Once you have made that decision, it is important for you to say, "I will not be moved from it."

Everyone was supposed to bow down to the idol, but Shadrach, Meshach, and Abednego would not. Nebuchadnezzar got the news, and those who told him said, "Some of the Jews won't bow down." Not all the Jews wouldn't bow down. There are some Christians who will bow down and compromise, and they will be the losers. But the young Israelite men said, "No, we will not bow down." Why could they do that? Because from the day they arrived, they purposed in their hearts. So they were taken to Nebuchadnezzar, and he was really angry with them. They were ruling over some of his major provinces, and they were setting a bad example. They were leadership!

Nebuchadnezzar said, "Don't you realize that if you don't bow down, I will throw you into the furnace?"

The three young Jewish men said, "Yes, we know it, but our God is able to deliver us from the fiery furnace and out of your hand."

God has two ways to deliver you in times of trial and temptation. He can deliver you from it (and I always like that better), or He can deliver you out of it (and I like that less). I think, *Lord, don't even let me go through it at all! Just take it away before it ever starts.* However, sometimes you have to go right into the middle of it, and it seems that at the very last minute, God rescues you out of it. But you must purpose in your heart that whether He delivers you from it or out of it, you will still not serve the devil. "If I have to go right into it and everyone at work hates me and says I am stupid and dumb, I am still proposing in my heart." If they all make fun of you and throw rocks at you, you still must purpose in your heart.

Well, God didn't deliver Daniel's three friends from it, so they were thrown into the furnace after they were bound with ropes. The furnace was so hot that the men who threw them in were burned to death, so there is no natural reason why these three men wouldn't be burned to death as well.

But something happened. The Bible says that when they got down there, the king could see into the furnace. How he could see, I don't know. That fiery furnace must have been deep in the earth like a pit, and he must have been able to look down into the flames. When he looked, he saw four men instead of three. He said, *"The fourth is like the Son of God"* (Daniel 3:25). If you have to go into the fire, Jesus is there with you.

There was something else very strange there. The Bible says that when they were thrown in, they were bound, but in Daniel 3:25 the ropes were loosed and they were walking around in the midst of the fire. The Babylonians were so shocked they said, "Even the fire has no power over them."

The satraps, administrators, governors, and the king's counselors gathered together, and they saw these men on whose bodies the fire had no power; the hair of their head was not singed nor were their garments affected, and the smell of fire was not on them. (Daniel 3:27)

This is the best verse in the whole story! God can put you in such a position that fire cannot burn or consume you. The way to be in that position is to purpose in your heart. You can go through the fire because He goes with you. They had purposed in their hearts, and they expressed it with their mouths and actions.

You must have faith that God can do the miraculous. Shadrach, Meshach, and Abednego had faith. They said, "Our God is able to deliver us." But faith is only the starting point.

> *But also for this very reason, giving all diligence, add to your faith virtue, to virtue knowledge, to knowledge self-control, to self-control perseverance, to perseverance godliness, to godliness brotherly kindness, and to brotherly kindness love. For if these things are yours and abound, you will be neither barren nor unfruitful in the knowledge of our Lord Jesus Christ.* (2 Peter 1:5–8)

The above passage says we are to add virtue to our faith. I was surprised at the meaning of virtue: it means praise. Add praise to your faith. It is important to praise and worship the Lord because it will keep you in faith.

Don't ever take it lightly in church services. Add to praise knowledge, then self-control, then patience, then godliness, then brotherly kindness, and then charity. If you abound in these, you will never be unfruitful in the knowledge of Jesus Christ.

The four Jewish men in our story had faith, and they praised God. They had knowledge of Him. They had self-control and didn't eat just anything. They were godly men with brotherly love. They had the love of God, and because of that, they were fruitful, and they didn't fall. If you purpose in your heart to live this way, you won't fall either, or if you fall, you will rise up again in His power; you'll be the head and not the tail.

Miracles and Deliverance are for Today

My daughter, Sarah, went to a Lutheran school. During her first year, she got into a big argument with her teacher about healing. He didn't believe in supernatural healing in the modern day. When she got home, she used Strong's concordance to be ready for the next day. She took this concordance with her for 10 days. On the 10th day, her teacher said, "Leave Strong's home."

She said, "Why?"

He answered, "Because I surrender."

"What do you mean, you surrender?" she asked.

He said, "I believe healing is for today."

One day, Sarah's teacher and his wife attended a meeting at our church and he received prayer for healing. That's not all that happened to him! He just happened to leave his children in our Sunday school. When his wife went to pick up their daughter, her Sunday school teacher said, "I have good news for you. Your daughter just received the baptism of the Holy Spirit with evidence of speaking in tongues."

Sarah said, "My head says, 'Oh, dear!' but my heart says, 'Whoopee!'" She went to school the next day, and her teacher invited us to dinner. She said, "Mother, do you think he wants to poison us?" Do you know what the topic of conversation was that evening? The baptism of the Holy Spirit. Don't compromise! Purpose in your heart to change circumstances; don't let them change you. You have a big God who will put you over the circumstances or the mountain in front of you. He will do the supernatural if you will make the stand in your heart.

After what happened in the fiery furnace, Nebuchadnezzar had to call the three Jewish men out. They wouldn't come out of their own accord. I don't blame them. Wouldn't you like to stay there with Jesus, too? Nebuchadnezzar said:

> *"Therefore I make a decree that any people, nation, or language which speaks anything amiss against the God of Shadrach, Meshach, and Abed-Nego shall be cut in pieces, and their houses shall be made an ash heap; because there is no other God who can deliver like this."* (Daniel 3:29)

There is no other God who can deliver like this! You serve the best! He wants you to be the best, too. It does not matter if you are a slave, a eunuch, or whatever. You may be the lowest in your office or the least popular in your room at school. You may think you are the ugliest and dumbest, but if you will purpose in your heart to serve the Lord, you won't be there long.

Nebuchadnezzar said, "He's the God of Shadrach, Meshach, and Abednego," but he didn't say, "He's my God." When he talked to Daniel, he called Him the God of gods, the Lord of kings, and the revealer of secrets, but he never said, "He's my God." The Lord changed Daniel's circumstances because he purposed in his heart, but sometimes more than circumstances need to be changed. Sometimes people need to be changed.

That's what God wants to do most of all: change people. He wants to come into their hearts. If you want to really flow in God, have a desire to see people changed, because that's God's desire. When you move in the desire to see alcoholics delivered, families brought together, and people transformed, you move in God. You will be a success because that is what God wants most of all. He loves people.

It looks like Nebuchadnezzar could never change. He was king of the world's greatest empire. Yes, he could have changed! Anybody can change. The worst kids can change! There was a boy in our Sunday school who used to pull a knife on the teacher. He went on to become a pastor and missionary. God knows how to change mean ones. He loves people!

Nebuchadnezzar wrote his testimony in Daniel 4. It is not only found in the Bible but also in historical records. It is found in Persian and Babylonian records because it was written by the king. He said, *"Peace be multiplied to you"* (v. 1).

Peace be multiplied to you? That sounds like something out of the New Testament! That is the way Paul wrote. It doesn't sound like a heathen king. He was cutting people's heads off and seizing weaker nations. Then he spoke of peace? What had happened to him?

He shared his testimony about a dream he had. In his dream, he saw a very big tree filled with birds. Then he saw the tree cut down to a short stump. Then he saw seven periods of time pass over, and he saw dew. He could not understand the dream and was very troubled by it, so he called for Daniel to interpret it. Remember, Daniel had purpose in his heart, was sitting in the gate of the king, was the master of the magicians, had divine wisdom, and was 10 times smarter than anyone else. That is why the king called for him.

Daniel interpreted the dream: "It is your kingdom. It will be taken from you, and you will be cut down to a stump. They will put a band of iron around you like a tree. Dew will fall upon it. Seven years of time will pass. What is sad is that you will live out in the wild. You will lose your mind if you don't get your heart right with God. I don't want this to happen to you, oh king" (Daniel 4:23–27, author's paraphrase).

Nebuchadnezzar didn't heed Daniel's warning, and one day he said, "Look at this great big kingdom I have built!" Within one hour after exalting himself, he went stark-raving mad. He was no longer a preserved earthen vessel; he became a crackpot. He cracked so badly that he thought he was an animal. How embarrassing to have a king act like an animal! So they left him out in the fields, and his son took his place on the throne.

I heard of a demon-possessed man who thought he was a crow. He would go to church and sit in the pew and "caw" just like a crow. He was a Jewish man — an intellectual man with a doctorate. In some way, he had become involved in witchcraft and the occult and decided he was a Native-American chief of the crow tribe.

His wife got saved and Spirit-filled and brought him to church. He was so bad that when he heard preaching about the blood of Jesus, he would go wild, and they would handcuff him. One time, when a visiting evangelist was at this church, the man was having his wife handcuff him before the services so he wouldn't embarrass her. The evangelist saw this happening in the back of the church and asked the pastor what was wrong with the man. The pastor answered, "He thinks he's a crow. He's possessed."

The evangelist went back, had them take the handcuffs off, took the man to a separate area, and dealt with him for six hours. He said, "Marilyn, I had no success.

It was just terrible. I prayed with him, cast the devil out, and came against the demon. I screamed at him until I was hoarse, and the demon in him was hoarse. I finally lost my voice and could only whisper. Then I said, 'Dear God, if I really have power in Jesus's name, then let this thing come out. If it doesn't, I'm going to throw in the towel.'" When he said that, the man was perfectly delivered and later became an elder in that church. He became a turned-on man for Jesus Christ! Praise the Lord!

When people choose the devil and his way and crash very badly, it is easy for me to say, "What's the use? I've given them Scripture, I've fasted and prayed with and for them, and they crash anyway." But the Lord showed me something in Job 14:7–9:

> *"For there is hope for a tree,*
> *If it is cut down, that it will sprout again,*
> *And that its tender shoots will not cease.*
> *Though its root may grow old in the earth,*
> *And its stump may die in the ground,*
> *Yet at the scent of water it will bud*
> *And bring forth branches like a plant."*

I find this encouraging because this is exactly what happened to Nebuchadnezzar. Do you know what the water is? The Holy Spirit. Just a little touch of the Holy Spirit and a person will say, "I don't have to stay like this! I can come out of it."

At the end of seven years, Nebuchadnezzar lifted his eyes and looked into heaven. Then his understanding returned to him. People of understanding praise the Lord; some people think we are the crazy ones, but we're not. We're the wise ones, because it is wise to praise the Lord. Nebuchadnezzar said, "*I blessed the Most High and praised and honored Him who lives forever: for His dominion is an everlasting dominion, and His kingdom is from generation to generation*" (Daniel 4:34). He was no longer a crackpot.

Do you see what happens? When people praise the Lord, they get better understanding. You can never praise the Lord enough. You could praise from now throughout eternity, and it would not be enough.

Nebuchadnezzar said something very important: "*I was restored to my kingdom, and excellent majesty was added to me*" (Daniel 4:36). God does not subtract from people. He adds to them. The devil is the one who subtracts good things from people.

From this story, not only do we see how four young men purposed in their hearts and changed their circumstances, but we see how it changed a king. Nebuchadnezzar was one of the greatest rulers that the world has ever known. Your circumstances and the people around you will be changed when you purpose in your heart to serve God.

Strategies for Winning

❶ *Determine What You Need to Be Delivered From*

Famine

To deliver their soul from death,
And to keep them alive in famine. (Psalm 33:19)

"I will deliver you from all your uncleannesses.
I will call for the grain and multiply it, and
bring no famine upon you." (Ezekiel 36:29)

✓ **Sin and Captivity**

"And now, Lord, what do I wait for?
My hope is in You.
Deliver me from all my transgressions;
Do not make me the reproach of the
  foolish." (Psalm 39:7–8)

Deliver me in Your righteousness,
  and cause me to escape.
Incline Your ear to me, and save me. (Psalm 71:2)

Help us, O God of our salvation,
For the glory of Your name;
And deliver us, and provide atonement for our sins,
For Your name's sake! (Psalm 79:9)

"Even the captives of the mighty
 shall be taken away,
And the prey of the terrible be delivered;
For I will contend with him who contends with you,
And I will save your children." (Isaiah 49:25)

He has delivered us from the power of
darkness and conveyed us into the kingdom
of the Son of His love. (Colossians 1:13)

Sickness, Disease, and Death

Return, O L<small>ORD</small>*, deliver me!*
Oh, save me for Your mercies' sake!
For in death there is no remembrance of You;
In the grave who will give You thanks? (Psalm 6:4–5)

For You have delivered my soul from death.
Have You not kept my feet from falling,

That I may walk before God
In the light of the living? (Psalm 56:13)

Surely He shall deliver you from
*   the snare of the fowler*
And from the perilous pestilence. (Psalm 91:3)

Difficult Situations and People

He delivered me from my strong enemy,
From those who hated me,
For they were too strong for me.
They confronted me in the day of my calamity,
But the L<small>ORD</small> *was my support.*
He also brought me out into a broad place;
He delivered me because He delighted
*   in me.* (Psalm 18:17–19)

Vindicate me, O God,
Plead my cause against an ungodly nation;
Oh, deliver me from the deceitful and unjust man!
For You are the God of my
*   strength. . . .* (Psalm 43:1–2)

Deliver me out of the mire,
And let me not sink;
Let me be delivered from those who hate me,
And out of the deep waters. (Psalm 69:14)

In my distress I cried to the L<small>ORD</small>,
And He heard me.
Deliver my soul, O L<small>ORD</small>, *from lying lips*
And from a deceitful tongue. (Psalm 120:1–2)

Fear and Distress

I sought the L<small>ORD</small>, *and He heard me,*
And delivered me from all my fears. (Psalm 34:4)

Then they cried out to the L<small>ORD</small> *in their trouble,*
And He delivered them out of their
 distresses. (Psalm 107:6)

❷ *Walk Out These Practical Action Steps*

Cry Out to God

They cried to You, and were delivered;
They trusted in You, and were not
 ashamed. (Psalm 22:5)

*Then I called upon the name of the L*ORD*:*
*"O L*ORD*, I implore You, deliver my soul!"*
*Gracious is the L*ORD*, and righteous;*
Yes, our God is merciful. (Psalm 116:4–5)

Trust God and Delight in Him

*"He trusted in the L*ORD*, let Him rescue Him;*
Let Him deliver Him, since He delights
 in Him!" (Psalm 22:8)

Keep my soul, and deliver me;
Let me not be ashamed, for I put my
 trust in You. (Psalm 25:20)

> *And the* LORD *shall help them and deliver them;*
> *He shall deliver them from the wicked,*
> *And save them,*
> *Because they trust in Him.* (Psalm 37:40)

Love God and Hate Evil

> *"Because he has set his love upon Me,*
> *therefore I will deliver him;*
> *I will set him on high, because he has*
> *known My name."* (Psalm 91:14)

> *You who love the* LORD, *hate evil!*
> *He preserves the souls of His saints;*
> *He delivers them out of the hand of*
> *the wicked.* (Psalm 97:10)

> *Consider my affliction and deliver me,*
> *For I do not forget Your law.* (Psalm 119:153)

Consider the Poor

> *Blessed is he who considers the poor;*
> *The* LORD *will deliver him in time*
> *of trouble.* (Psalm 41:1)

"Offer to God thanksgiving,
And pay your vows to the Most High.
Call upon Me in the day of trouble;
I will deliver you, and you shall glorify Me."
(Psalm 50:14–15)

Deliver the poor and needy;
Free them from the hand of the wicked.
(Psalm 82:4)

Seek God

I sought the Lord, *and He heard me,*
And delivered me from all my fears.
They looked to Him and were radiant,
And their faces were not ashamed.
This poor man cried out, and the Lord *heard him,*
And saved him out of all his troubles.
The angel of the Lord *encamps all*
    around those who fear Him,
And delivers them. (Psalm 34:4–7)

Take Refuge in God

The L<small>ORD</small> is my rock and my
fortress and my deliverer;
My God, my strength, in whom I will trust;
My shield and the horn of my salvation,
my stronghold. (Psalm 18:2)

I will say of the L<small>ORD</small>, "He is my
refuge and my fortress;
My God, in Him I will trust."
Surely He shall deliver you from
the snare of the fowler
And from the perilous pestilence.
He shall cover you with His feathers,
And under His wings you shall take refuge;
His truth shall be your shield and buckler.
(Psalm 91:2–4)

Worship God

Abraham and Isaac: Genesis 22
Joshua takes Jericho: Joshua 6
Job loses everything: Job 1:13–22
Daniel in Babylon: Daniel 6
The Leper and Jesus: Matthew 8:1–4

③ *Be Aware of How God Might Choose to Deliver You*

By His Hand

That Your beloved may be delivered,
Save with Your right hand, and hear me.
(Psalm 60:5)

Stretch out Your hand from above;
Rescue me and deliver me out of great waters . . .
(Psalm 144:7)

By His Word

He sent His word and healed them,
And delivered them from their destructions.
(Psalm 107:20)

Let my supplication come before You;
Deliver me according to Your word.
(Psalm 119:170)

By His Shelter

Deliver me, O Lord, from my enemies;
In You I take shelter. (Psalm 143:9)

My lovingkindness and my fortress,
My high tower and my deliverer,
My shield and the One in whom I take refuge . . .
(Psalm 144:2)

❹ Thank God for His Deliverance and Its Benefits

Praise

I will freely sacrifice to You;
I will praise Your name, O Lord, for it is good.
For He has delivered me out of all trouble;
And my eye has seen its desire upon
　　my enemies. (Psalm 54:6–7)

Peace

He has delivered my soul in peace from
 the battle that was against me,
For there were many against me. (Psalm 55:18)

Honor

"He shall call upon Me, and I will answer him;
I will be with him in trouble;
I will deliver him and honor him.
With long life I will satisfy him,
And show him My salvation." (Psalm 91:15–16)

2
———

Winning Against the Devil

Did you know that you can paralyze the devil? You can! And the reason that you can is because Jesus gave you complete authority over him. Many times, I've thought that the greatest compliment I could receive would be to be known in hell the way that Jesus and Paul were. I'd like to know that the devil says the same thing about me that he said about Jesus and Paul in Acts 19:13 and 15. In this account, there were seven sons of Sceva who were trying to cast out a devil from a certain man. They tried casting him out *"by the Jesus whom Paul preaches."* Do you know what that devil said to them? He said, *"Jesus I know, and Paul I know; but who are you?"* Just imagine it: Jesus and Paul were known in hell. Why? Not only because they had the authority to paralyze the devil, but because they used it.

To be known in hell can be dynamite. Think of this: you get up in the morning, and Satan says, "Oh no! There's that Christian getting up again, and I know that he's coming after me." I'd love that, because, although Satan would really like to paralyze believers, you can turn the tables on him because of Jesus's victory on the cross.

Satan's Number One Weapon

First of all, I want to tell you that Satan has a number-one weapon with which he attempts to paralyze God's people. That weapon is death.

When Satan tempted the very first man, Adam, to sin, his goal was to bring forth death. There are actually three kinds of death: spiritual, physical, and eternal.

Spiritual Death

In Genesis 2:17, God told Adam not to eat the fruit from the *"tree of the knowledge of good and evil,"* for if he did, he would *"surely die."* But Adam did not die physically when he ate that fruit. He died spiritually. Because of his sin, Adam was no longer alive to God; he was spiritually dead.

Eternal Death

Because of spiritual death, unless mankind becomes right with God through the perfect sacrifice of Jesus Christ on the cross, he experiences another type of death — the end result of being spiritually dead: eternal death. Satan and his demons were originally the only ones who were to taste eternal death. But now any person who is not alive to God through Jesus Christ will also face this type of death.

However, if you've been born again by accepting Jesus Christ as your Lord and Savior, you know that you aren't dead spiritually. You know that you'll never have to taste of eternal death because you have Jesus's life: eternal life. Therefore, the devil cannot work these two death principles within you. There is only one death principle with which he'll try to paralyze you as a Christian, and that is physical death!

Physical Death

Physical death is more than just the final death of your physical body. Physical death is the "slow death" process that Satan may use on your mind and your emotions. Physical death can also be sickness within your body. Consider what 1 John 3:14 says: *"He who does not love his brother abides in death."*

You could be a born-again child of God, but if you're not acting on Jesus's perfect law of love, death is at work within your physical body. This death will stop the blessings of God and leave you wide open for the devil's attacks. It may be in the form of sickness, or your mind and emotions could be depressed and troubled.

Romans 8:6 says that to be *"carnally minded is death."* Can a Christian be carnally minded? Certainly. In fact, hatred itself is carnal — a part of the old, sinful nature. What does carnality bring? Death. Satan wants to bring physical death into your life by trying to get you involved in carnality. He wants to paralyze God's blessings for you. God has seen ahead for you, though. He has already provided you with a way to destroy death and put a stop to the devil's weapons. You're going to be totally set free from the death principle when you discover it!

Destroying Satan's Weapon

Hebrews 2:14–15 offers a key about how Jesus has already set you free from the death principle:

> *Inasmuch then as the children have partaken of flesh and blood, He Himself likewise shared in the same, that through death He might destroy him who had the power of death, that is, the devil, and release those who through fear of death were all their lifetime subject to bondage.*

Jesus Christ has already taken death upon Himself so that He could destroy its power over you.

> *He was assigned a grave with the wicked,*
>   *and with the rich in his death,*
> *though he had done no violence, nor was any*
>   *deceit in his mouth.* (Isaiah 53:9 NIV)

After Jesus took every form of death upon Himself, He arose from the dead and destroyed its power over you. He did all of this because He wants you to have abundant life in Him! Satan wants to get you into a position to let him work the destructive principle of death on the inside, but you don't need to accept it. Jesus already took it for you.

There's another exciting thing about all that Jesus has done for you: He also released you from the fear of death! He knew that fear would hinder your walk with Him by keeping you in bondage. Jesus doesn't want His church in bondage; He wants you free! He wants you to be so free that you don't even have to fear death, much less have it working within you!

If Jesus destroyed death and the fear of it, why are so many Christians still fearful? If Jesus has set His people free from their old, carnal natures, why are so many still carnally minded? I asked the Lord, "Why does the body of Christ allow Satan's death principle to keep operating in their lives?"

He said, "Because they don't know what they already have in Jesus!" That's true! Hosea 4:6 says, *"My people are destroyed for lack of knowledge."* God doesn't want you to be destroyed. He wants you to have the knowledge to destroy the works of darkness.

Your Number One Weapon

In John 10:10, the Bible clearly states that Satan is a thief who only wants *"to steal, and to kill, and to destroy."* If Satan were to walk into your home today, what do you think he would want to steal? Would he try to steal your microwave? Your rug? No! Satan wants your valuables, and Psalm 19:10 states that the words of God *"are more desirable than gold, even the finest gold"* (NLT). The Word of God is your most valuable possession, and that's exactly what Satan wants to steal. You will find that the Word of God is your number one weapon, as well as your most valuable treasure, so it's no wonder that the devil wants to steal it!

How can he steal the Word from you? By causing you to forget! You may hear the Word over and over again; you may be reading it every day and memorizing Scripture, but you can still have trouble recalling it. That's because Satan wants you to forget what you've heard! Why does he want you to forget it? Because it is God's Word that gives you the authority to paralyze him!

Your very first step in paralyzing the devil is to take this cure for your memory from Psalm 119:11, which says, *"Your word I have hidden in my heart."* You can have perfect recall, and if you'll claim this Scripture, the devil will have to stop stealing the Word from your memory!

Using Your Weapon

You've found out that Jesus has already freed you from Satan's number one weapon: death. You've also learned that your most valuable possession is God's Word, and that is the weapon that you're going to use to stop death. Now that you know what your weapon is, which will paralyze the devil, you need to know how to use it!

Have you ever looked in the mirror and said, "I'm falling apart!" Have you ever felt that you were falling apart in your mind and emotions? Most people have. But even so, you never need to feel that way again. Jesus has a life principle for you, and it will cause you to overcome Satan's death principle. Proverbs 18:21 expresses it beautifully: *"Death and life are in the power of the tongue, and those who love it will eat its fruit."*

There it is! Using the "power of the tongue" is the only way that you're going to take hold of the authority that Jesus has given you. You can only use His life principle through the use of that small member, your tongue. Jesus's authority to destroy the devil will only come to you one way: by speaking it.

When you speak the Word, you will be affected mentally, emotionally, physically, and spiritually. God's Word is the power of life in your tongue, and speaking it will bring life into any situation that you have. Why? Because when you start agreeing with God, you're using His principle. He's already overcome every type of death for you.

Think about the time that the devil tempted Jesus in the wilderness (Matthew 4:1–11). Jesus was in the desert, and He'd been fasting for 40 days. At the end of the fast, the devil came to Him to tempt Him, and what did Jesus say? He said, *"It is written."* He spoke the Word of God.

Did the devil leave immediately? Did he say, "Ok, Jesus, that settles it. Goodbye." No! Sometimes the devil can be hard of hearing! He came back to tempt Jesus two more times, and each time that he returned, Jesus said, *"It is written."* He attacked the devil with the same weapon that you have to use in your own attacks: the Word of God. Jesus knew that the power of life was in His tongue, and He used it, both offensively and defensively!

Notice that when the devil came back again, Jesus didn't complain by saying, "I've been speaking the Word, and the devil still came back. This is supposed to work, but it's not working!" No! He stood firmly on the Word of God and said, *"It is written."*

When you tell the devil, "It is written," you'll begin to break his death principle in your life, but you had better count on speaking the Word more than once. Remember, Jesus had been fasting for 40 days; spiritually, He was very strengthened from it, but He still had to speak the Word three times! By speaking the Word every time the devil returns, you'll bring more life into your circumstances. Say, "It is written." Speak the Word!

You need to quote the Bible to the devil because he won't read. Tell him again and again, if you have to, and the same thing that happened with Jesus will happen with you: the devil will leave! But you've got to be more stubborn than he is.

When the devil left Jesus, something really beautiful happened, and it will be an encouragement to you. It is in Matthew 4:11, which says, *"Angels came and ministered to Him."* Isn't it exciting to know that God has special things prepared for His victorious children! I believe that when you defeat the devil, angels will come and rejoice with you! They'll minister to you. There are some very special benefits for those who will take up the weapon of God: His Word!

Revelation 12:11 says that Christians will overcome Satan *"by the blood of the Lamb and by the word of their testimony."* Your own strength is not sufficient. If you're trying to defeat the devil in any other way but by God's Word, you can be sure that he won't leave. You must make the choice; the power of death and life are in your tongue. If you'll start saying, "It is written," and then use a Bible verse that applies to your situation, what will happen? You'll be crushing Satan's death principle in your life!

Overcoming for the Future

Ecclesiastes 12 is a very unusual Scripture. When I studied it, I became aware that it actually describes the physical death process. You see, many people experience fear about entering old age, and that's not from God. That is fear of death, and Jesus has released you from that fear.

Have you ever been fearful of old age or death? If you have, you're going to be delivered from it! In fact, the Word of God has even said that Jesus has given you enough authority to name the day that you will die! There will be more about this later. First, look at Ecclesiastes 12:1:

> *Remember now your Creator in*
> *   the days of your youth,*
> *Before the difficult days come,*
> *And the years draw near when you say,*
> *"I have no pleasure in them."*

The very first verse of this chapter has given you a key to avoid the death principle, which can work during your later years: remember your Creator while you're young. If you're thinking, *Well, that's fine; I'll just have to keep this in mind as I get older*, you're going to be in for a big surprise. You should start speaking the Word now. The Word of God has been compared to a seed, and if you'll start planting that seed for your future by speaking it, you'll be able to harvest results when you need them. You can paralyze the devil for the years to come.

Let's continue in Ecclesiastes 12; you will see a picture of the aging process: *"In the day when the keepers of the house tremble, and the strong men bow down"* (v. 3). What are the keepers? They are the feet of an aged person, weak and trembling. The strong men in this verse are actually the person's knees, which have become unsteady through the death process of age. This is symbolism.

"When the grinders cease because they are few, and those that look through the windows grow dim" (v. 3). Here you can see that this person has lost most of his teeth (grinders); they are unable to chew the food that they once did. His eyes, portrayed as *"those that look through the windows,"* have grown dim with age.

"When the doors are shut in the streets, and the sound of grinding is low" (v. 4). The death process has affected the person by making them hard of hearing. Nearby sounds cannot be heard. In the next part of this verse, you will see another characteristic of the death process in age, which makes the person in this portrayal fearful: *"When one rises up at the sound of a bird, and all the daughters of music are brought low"* (v. 4).

Small sounds make this person nervous and afraid. His voice has also grown weak. Can you see what the author of this book is showing? He goes on to say that this person is also fearful about falling, another trait which often applies to elderly people, to whom falls can be devastating. Finally, in this next verse you will also see the one thing which is flowering: *"Also they are afraid of height, and of terrors in the way; when the almond tree blossoms . . ."* (v. 5). When an almond tree is in bloom, it is white. This imagery portrays an aged person with flourishing white hair.

"The grasshopper is a burden, and desire fails. For man goes to his eternal home, and the mourners go about the streets" (v. 5). What has been shown? This is the picture of a man undergoing the death process of age. The Word of God has set it forth, step by step.

Could this difficult aging process have been avoided? I believe that if this person had remembered his Creator in his youth, his later days would not have been "difficult days," and he could have had "pleasure in them."

God wants your best days to be your last days! When He took Moses home, Moses was 120 years old, and the Bible says that *"His eyes were not dim nor his natural vigor diminished"* (Deuteronomy 34:7). Why? Because he remembered his Creator in his early days. Moses paralyzed the death process, and because he clung to the life process (God's Word), death could not work in him. If ever a man spoke the Word of God, I'm sure it was Moses; after all, he wrote the first five books of the Bible.

I can just imagine God speaking His Word to Moses, and then Moses speaking it to the people. I'm sure that when you can repeat Genesis, Exodus, Leviticus,

Numbers, and Deuteronomy by heart, you'll look young, too! Where is the power of life and death? It's in your tongue. When you start speaking the Word, you're remembering your Creator, and His Word will be the life in you that will keep you young!

Abraham was 100 years old when he became a father. I'd say that's pretty impressive. Have you heard of anyone lately who became a father at age 100? What did Abraham do? He remembered his Creator in his youth. He didn't stagger at God's promise; he spoke it.

And Sarah? Well, she was 90 years old when she had Isaac. *"By faith Sarah herself also received strength to conceive seed, and she bore a child when she was past the age, because she judged Him faithful who had promised"* (Hebrews 11:11). The word "strength" in this verse means "miracle working power." The same Word that created a youth-life process in Sarah's body will do the same thing for you: it will keep you young!

Has your body been attacked by Satan's death process? If so, start reversing his process and paralyzing him by speaking the Word of God! Use your number one weapon on him, because God wants every year to be your best ever, and every year will be your best when you use His life principle.

Until You're Satisfied

I want to tell you about Abraham's death. When he died, the Bible doesn't say that he had diabetes, arthritis, or any other disease. Scripture says that Abraham just gathered up his feet and went to be with his people; he didn't die a miserable death. He made the decision to die, picked up his feet, and went to be with the people whose deaths had preceded his. Abraham, who was called the Father of Faith, didn't just live in faith — he died in it, and so can you.

Stephen was a beautiful deacon who really preached a sermon to the Pharisees before his death. You'll find his account in Acts 6 and 7. The Pharisees were getting ready to stone him, and Stephen just stood firmly and preached the Word to them about the beginning of Jewish history, right up to God's dealing with them. He was speaking words of life, so you can imagine that he was filled with the pure life of God when they began stoning him. Did they stone him to death? No! Stephen was full of the life of God's Word. That life started shining from his countenance, until he looked like an angel. Then he looked up and saw Jesus standing next to the Father, and he said, *"Lord Jesus, receive my spirit"* (Acts 7:59). Stephen died in faith!

Simeon, the man who came into the temple when Jesus was dedicated by His mother, named the day of his death. The story is found in Luke 2:29–30, and this is what he said: *"Lord, now You are letting Your servant depart in peace, according to Your word; for my eyes have seen Your salvation."* He said, "I'm ready to die, for I've finally seen the Messiah." Simeon named his death day.

Another person to name the day of his death was the apostle Paul. Paul told the church at Philippi, "I'd love to die, because then I could be with the Lord. But it's better for you that I stay around, so I'll stay." He spoke as if the choice was his, and it was! At this particular time, Paul stayed, but when the time came for him to go and be with the Lord, he wrote, *"The time of my departure is at hand"* (2 Timothy 4:6). Paul was satisfied with his life, and so he was satisfied to name the day of his death and be with the Lord. He'd run the race; he'd fought the fight; and it was time to go.

Psalm 91:16 says that the Lord will satisfy you with long life. In this context, I think "satisfy" means that as long as you're satisfied to live, God will let you live.

Then, when you've been satisfied and are ready to die and be with Him, God will let you come be with Him.

God gave you authority over hell and death through Jesus Christ. He wants you to live abundantly until you've been satisfied! Speak life (His Word) to your body, mind, and emotions. You could, by the same token, speak death, but why? Many people don't realize that when they walk around speaking negatively, they are abiding in death. They are inviting an early death. The choice is yours. You can yield your tongue in any direction that you choose, but if you're yielding it to carnality, remember that you're yielding it to death.

One time a woman came up for prayer after a service, and when she knelt down, she let loose that eerie scream of a demon-oppressed person. She was carrying on and saying terrible things, and many people were praying for her. I rushed over and rebuked the devil, commanding him to leave, but nothing happened. We persisted for quite some time, with no success in liberating her of the oppression.

Then, I asked the Lord what was wrong, and I asked Him to show me how to pray for her. He said, "Tell her to tell the devil to go." I told her to do this, and she replied, "I can't." Then, the Lord told me to be very firm with her, and I said, "Then leave here with that devil!" Instantly, she screamed out, "Go, in Jesus's name!" In a split second, that girl was totally in control of all her faculties and completely coherent.

Later, she came in for counseling and said that she'd been saved and Spirit-filled for about six months, but she had once been in the occult and had had dealings with the devil. Periodically, the devil would come against her, and she would have these reactions. "But," she said, "I didn't know that I had authority over him! He'll never do that to me again." From that time on, she paralyzed the devil. She spoke the Word, and rebuked the devil in the name of Jesus, and he had to leave her alone!

I know of another young man whom we met one year while we were on a teaching cruise. One afternoon, he said, "Marilyn, I never read my Bible." I said, "What do you mean by that?" He told me, "I can't read it because the devil won't let me. Every time I open my Bible, the devil comes in and harasses me so that I can't read. He is tormenting me." We began going through the Scriptures together, and I showed him that Jesus had given him *"the authority to trample on serpents and scorpions, and over all the power of the enemy, and nothing shall by any means hurt*

[him]" (Luke 10:19). He said, "Do you mean that I can tell the devil where to go?" He was astonished!

That night, he came to dinner and said, "Do you know what I did this afternoon? I told the devil to 'get,' and he 'got!'" Praise the Lord! This young man found out that Jesus gave him authority over the devil, and he used it! He spoke the final authority of God's Word out of his mouth and paralyzed the devil!

Freedom From Death

Return to Ecclesiastes 12:6–7, which says:

> *Remember your Creator before*
> *   the silver cord is loosed,*
> *Or the golden bowl is broken,*
> *Or the pitcher shattered at the fountain,*
> *Or the wheel broken at the well.*
> *Then the dust will return to the earth as it was,*
> *And the spirit will return to God who gave it.*

What does all of this mean? In his commentary, Matthew Henry remarks on this passage, saying:

v. 6 Then shall the silver cord, by which soul and body were wonderfully fastened together, be loosed, that the sacred knot untied; the golden bowl, which held the waters of life for us, be broken; then shall the pitcher with which we used to fetch up water, for the constant support of life and the repair of its decays, be broken, even at the fountain, so that it can fetch up no more; and the wheel (all those organs that serve for the collecting and distributing of nourishment) shall be broken, and disabled to do their office any more. The body shall become like a watch when the spring is broken, the motion of all the wheels is stopped and they all stand still. Death will resolve us into our first principles.

v. 7 Man is a strange sort of creature, a ray of heaven united to a clod of earth; at death these are separated, and each goes to the place whence it came. The body, that clod of clay, returns to its own earth. The soul, that beam of light returns to that God who, when he made man of the dust of the ground, breathed into him the breath of life, to make him a living soul (Gen. ii. 7). The soul does not die with the body; it is redeemed from the power of the grave (Ps. xlix. 15); it can subsist without it and will in a state of separation from it, as the candle burns, and burns brighter, when it is taken out of the dark lantern.

Jesus overcame death, He loosed any bondages and cords of death which were over you. He loosed you from its fear, and gave you a robe of His own righteousness! He now holds the keys of authority over death, and He says, *"Whatever you bind on earth will be bound in heaven, and whatever you loose on earth will be loosed in heaven"* (Matthew 18:18).

You may be born again and have passed from spiritual death into spiritual life. You may know for certain that you have eternal life, but have you been allowing Satan to bring death into any area of your life? Perhaps you've allowed him to keep you in bondage to a habit; maybe you've been thinking and speaking carnally; perhaps your body is sick. Whatever the case, Jesus wants to minister life to you in every area of your life!

Whatever it is that you need, rejoice! Jesus has already given you the provision: His Word! He came to give you life in His abundance (John 10:10), and He's already given you your freedom. Now, you just need to take it. Take the authority of Jesus by saying, "It is written!" Are you ready to experience long life in His abundance? You're sure to step out victoriously, carrying the keys to the kingdom and wearing the robe of righteousness. Go paralyze the devil!

Strategies for Winning

In the beginning, Satan was known as Lucifer and was glorious to behold, created by God as an angel of praise. However, he tried to take God's throne and lost God's glory. Since then, the devil has dedicated himself to opposing God. He tempts us to sin, then casts blame on our character.

The devil also casts doubt on who God is, and he aims at pulling down the kingdom of God. The devil has no compassion. His power is used only for evil to destroy everything good. He destroys in order to show his own power. It is important to remember, however, that Satan is not all-powerful. You can use the practical strategies below to overcome the devil's schemes.

❶ Understand These Three Things

There are three things that are of the utmost importance for you to understand and act on as you wage battles against the devil.

1. Know that God has already won the war. *"Having disarmed principalities and powers, He [Jesus] made*

a public spectacle of them, triumphing over them in it" (Colossians 2:15).

2. Realize that Jesus has given you power over the devil and his demons. *". . . On this rock I will build My church, and the gates of Hades shall not prevail against it"* (Matthew 16:18).

3. Praise God for the victory He has arranged in advance for His people. *"And I saw something like a sea of glass mingled with fire, and those who have the victory over the beast, over his image and over his mark and over the number of his name, standing on the sea of glass, having harps of God"* (Revelation 15:2).

❷ Recognize the Devil and His Strategies

Learn to recognize the character of the devil and use the weapons God has formed against him. The devil has perfected his techniques over the years. He hopes to defeat you by keeping you ignorant of how he works. Learn to avoid devilish traps and let God show you how to deal with every evil trait. If you become aware of his strategy, you can win!

1. The devil is proud (Jeremiah 49:16). Defeat his pride by rejoicing in Jesus's triumph over him! *"Now thanks be to God who always leads us in triumph in Christ, and through us diffuses the fragrance of His knowledge in every place"* (2 Corinthians 2:14).

2. The devil is powerful (Ephesians 2:2). Confess God's authority over Satan and his demons! What a word this is! *"For with authority and power He commands the unclean spirits, and they come out"* (Luke 4:36).

3. The devil is wicked (Matthew 13:38–39). Remember that Jesus has obtained everlasting victory over wickedness. *"To him who overcomes I will grant to sit with Me on My throne, as I also overcame and sat down with My Father on His throne"* (Revelation 3:21).

4. The devil intends evil in all his ways (Isaiah 59:7). Realize that God is the maker of good things. *"Every good gift and every perfect gift is from above, and comes down from the Father of lights, with whom there is no variation or shadow of turning"* (James 1:17).

5. The devil is subtle (Genesis 3:1). Outsmart him by developing a firm foundation of Scripture. *"If you continue in your faith, established and firm, and do not move from the hope held out in the gospel"* (Colossians 1:23 NIV).

6. The devil is deceitful (Psalm 36:3–4). Use God's truth to overturn Satan's lies. *"You shall know the truth, and the truth shall make you free"* (John 8:32).

7. The devil is fierce (Revelation 13:2). Realize that God has compassion on His people. *"For if you return to the LORD, your brethren and your children will be treated with compassion by those who lead them captive, so that they may come back to this land; for the LORD your God is gracious and merciful, and will not turn His face from you if you return to Him"* (2 Chronicles 30:9).

8. The devil is a murderer (John 8:44). Remember that God is the creator and giver of life. *"All things were made through Him, and without Him nothing was made that was made. In Him was life, and the life was the light of men"* (John 1:3–4).

9. The devil is destructive (Psalm 119:95). Recognize the mighty power of God to restore. *"So I will restore to you the years that the swarming locust has eaten . . ."* (Joel 2:25).

10. The devil is an accuser (Revelation 12:10). Go to Jesus as your advocate before the Father. *". . . If anyone sins, we have an Advocate with the Father, Jesus Christ the righteous"* (1 John 2:1).

11. The devil is a seducer (1 Timothy 4:1). *". . . God is faithful, who will not allow you to be tempted beyond what you are able, but with the temptation will also make the way of escape, that you may be able to bear it"* (1 Corinthians 10:13).

12. The devil is an oppressor (Luke 13:16). Use the power of the Holy Spirit to throw off Satan's oppression. *"God anointed Jesus of Nazareth with the Holy Spirit and with power, who went about doing good and healing all who were oppressed by the devil, for God was with Him"* (Acts 10:38).

13. The devil is king over the demons (Revelation 9:11). Operate in the power of God's grace to be greater than the demonic realm. *"Now I know that the LORD is greater than all the gods"* (Exodus 18:11).

14. The devil masquerades as good (2 Corinthians 11:14), so be cautious. *"Beloved, do not believe every spirit, but test the spirits, whether they are of God; because many false prophets have gone out into the world"* (1 John 4:1).

15. The devil works false wonders (2 Thessalonians 2:9). Therefore, believe only the Word of God. *"As for you, let that abide in you which you heard from the beginning. If what you heard from the beginning abides in you, you also will abide in the Son and in the Father"* (1 John 2:24 NASB).

16. The devil tries to hinder God's people (Daniel 10:11–13). You will need to stay focused. *"I press toward the goal for the prize of the upward call of God in Christ Jesus"* (Philippians 3:14).

17. The devil makes war on Christians (Revelation 12:17), so take up God's spiritual weapons. *"For the weapons of our warfare are not carnal but mighty in God for pulling down strongholds"* (2 Corinthians 10:4).

18. The devil opposes God's work (Zechariah 3:1), be strong. *"Be strong and of good courage, do not fear nor be afraid of them; for the Lord your God, He is the One*

who goes with you. He will not leave you nor forsake you" (Deuteronomy 31:6).

19. The devil blinds the world to the truth of the gospel (2 Corinthians 4:4). Therefore, keep your eyes open. *"But blessed are your eyes for they see, and your ears for they hear"* (Matthew 13:16).

20. The devil causes sickness and disease (Matthew 4:24). Use God's Word to strengthen your body. *"He sent His word and healed them, and delivered them from their destructions"* (Psalm 107:20).

21. The devil is the father of lies (John 8:44), make sure you learn the truth. *"Teach me Your way, O Lord; I will walk in Your truth; unite my heart to fear Your name"* (Psalm 86:11).

22. The devil tries to snare you (1 Timothy 3:7), so use wisdom and discernment in your behavior. *"I want you to be wise about what is good, and innocent about what is evil"* (Romans 16:19 NIV).

23. The devil causes you to be troubled (1 Samuel 16:14). You will need to abide in the peace of God. *"He has redeemed my soul in peace from the battle that was against me, for there were many against me"* (Psalm 55:18).

24. The devil steals, kills, and destroys (John 10:10). So be on guard and alert. *"He who scatters has come up before your face. Man the fort! Watch the road! Strengthen your flanks! Fortify your power mightily"* (Nahum 2:1).

25. The devil perverts Scripture (Acts 13:10). Therefore, be strong in the Word. *"The wicked have laid a snare for me, yet I have not strayed from Your precepts"* (Psalm 119:110).

26. Evil will increase in the last days (2 Timothy 3:1–5, 13). Pay attention to the signs of the times. *"Therefore rejoice, O heavens, and you who dwell in them! Woe to the inhabitants of the earth and the sea! For the devil has come down to you, having great wrath, because he knows that he has a short time"* (Revelation 12:12).

③ *Avoid the Work of the Devil*

When you are born again, a new nature is born into your spirit. Your old nature often doesn't want to let go of past habits, thoughts, and speech. God's Word will help you triumph over old ways.

1. Don't sin when you are angry. *"'Be angry, and do not sin': do not let the sun go down on your wrath, nor give place to the devil"* (Ephesians 4:26–27).

2. Avoid illicit/illegal drugs and alcohol. *"Do not be drunk with wine, in which is dissipation; but be filled with the Spirit"* (Ephesians 5:18).

3. Avoid bitterness. *"Let all bitterness, wrath, anger, clamor, and evil speaking be put away from you, with all malice"* (Ephesians 4:31).

4. Avoid the works of the flesh. *"Have no fellowship with the unfruitful works of darkness, but rather expose them"* (Ephesians 5:11).

5. Avoid the occult. *"There shall not be found among you anyone who makes his son or his daughter pass through the fire, or one who practices witchcraft, or a soothsayer, or one who interprets omens, or a sorcerer"* (Deuteronomy 18:10).

6. Avoid Christians who willfully sin. *"I wrote to you in my epistle not to keep company with sexually immoral people. Yet I certainly did not mean with the sexually immoral people of this world, or with the covetous, or extortioners, or idolaters, since then you would need to go out of the world. But now I have written to you not to keep company with anyone named a brother, who is sexually immoral, or covetous, or an idolater, or a reviler, or a drunkard, or an extortioner — not even to eat with such a person"* (1 Corinthians 5:9–11).

7. Avoid strife. *"Now I urge you, brethren, note those who cause divisions and offenses, contrary to the doctrine which you learned, and avoid them"* (Romans 16:17).

❹ Remember That the Devil Will be Judged by God

Satan is no longer in God's favor. He chose to disobey God. God judges disobedience — having the authority to punish all evildoers — and He has prepared a place of torment for the devil.

1. Recognize that Satan fell from an exalted position. *"How you are fallen from heaven, O Lucifer, son of the* *morning! How you are cut down to the ground, you who weakened the nations!"* (Isaiah 14:12).

2. Know that Satan willfully disobeyed God. *"I will ascend into heaven, I will exalt my throne above the stars of God; I will also sit on the mount of the congregation on the farthest sides of the north; I will ascend above the heights of the clouds, I will be like the Most High"* (Isaiah 14:13–14).

3. Remember that God has a place of judgment prepared for Satan. *"But you are brought down to the realm of the dead, to the depths of the pit"* (Isaiah 14:15 NIV).

4. Realize that the devil knows his end. *"The devil, who deceived them, was cast into the lake of fire and brimstone where the beast and the false prophet are. And they will be tormented day and night forever and ever"* (Revelation 20:10).

5. Understand that fallen angels — Satan's demons — will share in his punishment. *"The angels who did not keep their proper domain, but left their own abode, He has reserved in everlasting chains under darkness for the judgment of the great day"* (Jude 1:6).

⑤ Walk With God in All Your Ways

Don't wait for Satan to attack. Take proactive steps to defeat his kingdom. Follow the Word of God and study His commands.

1. Listen for God's voice. *"But if you indeed obey His voice and do all that I speak, then I will be an enemy to your enemies and an adversary to your adversaries"* (Exodus 23:22).

2. Walk in God's abundance. *"You shall remember the LORD your God, for it is He who gives you power to get wealth, that He may establish His covenant which He swore to your fathers, as it is this day"* (Deuteronomy 8:18).

3. Claim your heritage that will keep you from the devil's destruction. *"No weapon formed against you shall prosper, and every tongue which rises against you in judgment you shall condemn. This is the heritage of the servants of the LORD, and their righteousness is from Me"* (Isaiah 54:17).

⑥ Learn the Powerful Ways God Has Given You to Fight the Devil

As spiritual warfare increases, God will direct you by His Word. God has given offensive and defensive weaponry to His army. Use them wisely.

1. Win through love and prayer. *"Love your enemies, bless those who curse you, do good to those who hate you, and pray for those who spitefully use you and persecute you"* (Matthew 5:44).

2. Minister grace to others. *"Let no corrupt word proceed out of your mouth, but what is good for necessary edification, that it may impart grace to the hearers"* (Ephesians 4:29).

3. Fight the good fight of faith. *"Fight the good fight of faith, lay hold on eternal life, to which you were also called and have confessed the good confession in the presence of many witnesses"* (1 Timothy 6:12).

4. Take your thoughts captive to God's will. *"For the weapons of our warfare are not carnal but mighty in God for pulling down strongholds, casting down arguments and every high thing that exalts itself against the knowledge of*

God, bringing every thought into captivity to the obedience of Christ" (2 Corinthians 10:4–5).

5. Have faith in the Word of God. *"Sanctify them by Your truth. Your word is truth"* (John 17:17).

6. Thank God for His wonderful works. *"For this reason we also thank God without ceasing, because when you received the word of God which you heard from us, you welcomed it not as the word of men, but as it is in truth, the word of God, which also effectively works in you who believe"* (1 Thessalonians 2:13).

7. Avoid Satan's traps and temptations. *"Flee also youthful lusts; but pursue righteousness, faith, love, peace with those who call on the Lord out of a pure heart"* (2 Timothy 2:22).

8. Stay attached to the branch of power — Jesus Christ. *"As you therefore have received Christ Jesus the Lord, so walk in Him, rooted and built up in Him and established in the faith, as you have been taught, abounding in it with thanksgiving"* (Colossians 2:6–7).

⑦ *Believe That the Battle is the Lord's*

The devil's real battle is with God. When you accepted Jesus Christ, you became a soldier in God's army. You train at the hands of the greatest general ever! The Lord leads as you fight the enemy. Rely on the name of Jesus and His power.

1. Don't be afraid. You're not alone — it is God's battle. *"'Do not fear or be dismayed because of this great multitude, for the battle is not yours but God's. . . . You need not fight in this battle; take your position, stand and watch the salvation of the LORD in your behalf, Judah and Jerusalem.' Do not fear or be dismayed; tomorrow, go out to face them, for the LORD is with you"* (2 Chronicles 20:15, 17 NASB).

2. Let God train you in righteous warfare. *"Blessed be the LORD my Rock, who trains my hands for war, and my fingers for battle"* (Psalm 144:1).

3. Ask God to cause you to triumph in every battle. *"O my God, I trust in You; let me not be ashamed; let not my enemies triumph over me"* (Psalm 25:2).

4. Be confident in God's power. *"Though an army may encamp against me, my heart shall not fear; though war may rise against me, in this I will be confident"* (Psalm 27:3).

5. Don't fight alone — fight through God! *"Through God we will do valiantly, for it is He who shall tread down our enemies"* (Psalm 108:13).

6. Use God's strength — you are the work of His hands. *"For You have armed me with strength for the battle; you have subdued under me those who rose up against me"* (Psalm 18:39).

7. Recognize the leader of the battle — God is the king of glory and victory. *"Who is this King of glory? The Lord strong and mighty, the Lord mighty in battle"* (Psalm 24:8).

8. Remember that God helps us subdue our enemies. *"For the Lord Most High is awesome; He is a great King over all the earth. He will subdue the peoples under us, and the nations under our feet. He will choose our inheritance for us, the excellence of Jacob whom He loves. Selah"* (Psalm 47:2–4).

9. Allow God to keep you in the place of victory. *"Cast your burden on the LORD, and He shall sustain you; He shall never permit the righteous to be moved"* (Psalm 55:22).

10. Expect God to give you wisdom for the fight. *"If any of you lacks wisdom, let him ask of God, who gives to all liberally and without reproach, and it will be given to him"* (James 1:5).

11. Remember that God battles with you against the enemy. *"For the LORD your God is He who goes with you, to fight for you against your enemies, to save you"* (Deuteronomy 20:4).

12. Ask God for spiritual strength. *"Trust in the LORD forever, for the LORD, the LORD himself, is the Rock eternal. He humbles those who dwell on high, he lays the lofty city low; he levels it to the ground and casts it down to the dust"* (Isaiah 26:4–5 NIV).

13. Remember that God fights on your behalf. *"Our God will fight for us"* (Nehemiah 4:20).

14. Realize that your battle is not for the kingdoms of this world. *"Jesus answered, 'My kingdom is not of this world. If My kingdom were of this world, My servants would fight, so that I should not be delivered to the Jews; but now My kingdom is not from here'"* (John 18:36).

15. Be valiant in the fight. *"For the time would fail me to tell of Gideon and Barak and Samson and Jephthah, also of David and Samuel and the prophets: who through faith subdued kingdoms, worked righteousness, obtained promises, stopped the mouths of lions, quenched the violence of fire, escaped the edge of the sword, out of weakness were made strong, became valiant in battle, turned to flight the armies of the aliens"* (Hebrews 11:32–34).

16. Do not fear the danger of battle. *"You shall not be afraid of the terror by night, nor of the arrow that flies by day, nor of the pestilence that walks in darkness, nor of the destruction that lays waste at noonday. A thousand may fall at your side, and ten thousand at your right hand; but it shall not come near you"* (Psalm 91:5–7).

17. Do not fear the power of the enemy. *"Do not be afraid, nor be dismayed; be strong and of good courage, for thus the*

LORD *will do to all your enemies against whom you fight"* (Joshua 10:25).

18. Ask God for the knowledge to fight well. *"Plans are established by counsel; by wise counsel wage war"* (Proverbs 20:18).

19. Know that the devil cannot resist the power of the name of Jesus. *"Lord, even the demons are subject to us in Your name"* (Luke 10:17).

20. Realize that the devil must obey Jesus Christ. *"For with authority He commands even the unclean spirits, and they obey Him"* (Mark 1:27).

21. Believe that Jesus gives you the power to exorcize demons. *"In My name they will cast out demons . . ."* (Mark 16:17).

22. Praise Jesus for paying the penalty of sin. *"John saw Jesus coming toward him, and said, 'Behold! The Lamb of God who takes away the sin of the world!'"* (John 1:29).

23. Realize that Jesus destroyed the power of death. *"He too shared in their humanity so that by his death he might break the power of him who holds the power of death — that is, the devil"* (Hebrews 2:14 NIV).

24. Let Jesus help you destroy the works of the devil. *"For this purpose the Son of God was manifested, that He might destroy the works of the devil"* (1 John 3:8).

25. Allow Jesus's blood to speak victory for you. *"And they overcame him by the blood of the Lamb and by the word of their testimony, and they did not love their lives to the death"* (Revelation 12:11).

26. Remember that God's love for you is greater than Satan's hatred. *"For God so loved the world that He gave His only begotten Son, that whoever believes in Him should not perish but have everlasting life"* (John 3:16).

27. Allow Jesus to complete what is lacking in you. *"You are complete in Him, who is the head of all principality and power"* (Colossians 2:10).

28. See Christ as the life in you. *"When Christ who is our life appears, then you also will appear with Him in glory"* (Colossians 3:4).

8 Have Faith When All Seems Lost

At times, the battle may seem so intense that you think all is lost. God's peace will be with you even on the most stressful occasions.

1. Enjoy God's rest and peace in the land of the enemy. *"But you will cross the Jordan and settle in the land the LORD your God is giving you as an inheritance, and he will give you rest from all your enemies around you so that you will live in safety"* (Deuteronomy 12:10 NIV).

2. Keep your peace in the middle of the battle. *"He has redeemed my soul in peace from the battle that was against me, for there were many against me"* (Psalm 55:18).

3. Do not be terrified by the circumstances. *"Hear, O Israel: Today you are on the verge of battle with your enemies. Do not let your heart faint, do not be afraid, and do not tremble or be terrified because of them; for the LORD your God is He* *who goes with you, to fight for you against your enemies, to save you"* (Deuteronomy 20:3–4).

4. Chase the enemy in the midst of his attack. *"The Lord will cause your enemies who rise against you to be defeated before your face; they shall come out against you one way and flee before you seven ways"* (Deuteronomy 28:7).

5. Know that the Lord will pay back Satan for persecution of believers. *"Also the Lord your God will put all these curses on your enemies and on those who hate you, who persecuted you"* (Deuteronomy 30:7).

6. Realize that your enemies cannot stand before God. *"The Lord gave them rest all around, according to all that He had sworn to their fathers. And not a man of all their enemies stood against them; the Lord delivered all their enemies into their hand"* (Joshua 21:44).

7. Remember that Satan cannot stand the presence of a faithful follower of God. *"Therefore submit to God. Resist the devil and he will flee from you"* (James 4:7).

⑨ Meditate on These Scriptures of Victory

Repeat these and let them become part of your arsenal. God will lead you to total victory.

> *They surrounded me,*
> *Yes, they surrounded me;*
> *But in the name of the L*ORD *I will destroy them.*
> *They surrounded me like bees;*
> *They were quenched like a fire of thorns;*
> *For in the name of the L*ORD *I will destroy them.*
> *You pushed me violently, that I might fall,*
> *But the L*ORD *helped me.*
> *The L*ORD *is my strength and song,*
> *And He has become my salvation.*
> *The voice of rejoicing and salvation*
> *Is in the tents of the righteous;*
> *The right hand of the L*ORD *does valiantly.*
> *The right hand of the L*ORD *is exalted;*
> *The right hand of the L*ORD *does valiantly.*
> (Psalm 118:11–16)

The Lord is your keeper;
The Lord is your shade at your right hand.
The sun shall not strike you by day,
Nor the moon by night.
The Lord shall preserve you from all evil;
He shall preserve your soul.
The Lord shall preserve your going
   out and your coming in
From this time forth, and even
   forevermore. (Psalm 121:5–8)

Our help is in the name of the Lord,
Who made heaven and earth. (Psalm 124:8)

For behold, the darkness shall cover the earth,
And deep darkness the people;
But the Lord will arise over you,
And His glory will be seen upon you. (Isaiah 60:2)

Finally, my brethren, be strong in the Lord and in the power of His might. Put on the whole armor of God, that you may be able to stand against the wiles of the devil. For we do not wrestle against flesh and blood, but against principalities, against powers, against the rulers of the darkness of this age, against spiritual hosts of wickedness in the heavenly places. Therefore take up the whole armor of God, that you may be able to withstand in the evil day, and having done all, to stand.

Stand therefore, having girded your waist with truth, having put on the breastplate of righteousness, and having shod your feet with the preparation of the gospel of peace; above all, taking the shield of faith with which you will be able to quench all the fiery darts of the wicked one. And take the helmet of salvation, and the sword of the Spirit, which is the word of God; praying always with all prayer and supplication in the Spirit, being watchful to this end with all perseverance and supplication for all the saints — and for me, that utterance may be given to me, that I may open my mouth boldly to make known the mystery of the gospel, for which I am an ambassador in chains; that in it I may speak boldly, as I ought to speak. (Ephesians 6:10–20)

"Because you have kept My command to persevere, I also will keep you from the hour of trial which shall come upon the whole world, to test those who dwell on the earth." (Revelation 3:10)

⑩ Enjoy the Spoils of Victory

Jesus won the greatest battle against the devil when He gave His life willingly on the cross. Jesus gained back what man lost, and Satan was defeated for eternity. God wants to give His warriors the spoils of victory. You have a part in winning souls for God's kingdom. Rejoice in God's favor.

1. Participate in every godly victory. *"The share of the man who stayed with the supplies is to be the same as that of him who went down to the battle. All will share alike"* (1 Samuel 30:24 NIV).

2. Take possession of what the enemy tried to keep from you. *"You may use the plunder the Lord your God gives you from your enemies"* (Deuteronomy 20:14 NIV).

3. Accept your heavenly reward. *"Praise be to the God and Father of our Lord Jesus Christ! In his great mercy he has*

given us new birth into a living hope through the resurrection of Jesus Christ from the dead, and into an inheritance that can never perish, spoil or fade. This inheritance is kept in heaven for you" (1 Peter 1:3–4 NIV).

4. Receive your anointing from God. *"You prepare a table before me in the presence of my enemies; you anoint my head with oil; my cup runs over"* (Psalm 23:5).

5. Realize that you are seated in heavenly places. *"But God, who is rich in mercy, because of His great love with which He loved us, even when we were dead in trespasses, made us alive together with Christ (by grace you have been saved), and raised us up together, and made us sit together in the heavenly places in Christ Jesus"* (Ephesians 2:4–6).

6. Thank God for great victory. *"Now to Him who is able to do exceedingly abundantly above all that we ask or think, according to the power that works in us"* (Ephesians 3:20).

7. Know that you have the mind of Christ. *"But we have the mind of Christ"* (1 Corinthians 2:16).

8. Recognize that you have been rescued from darkness. *"He has delivered us from the power of darkness and conveyed us into the kingdom of the Son of His love"* (Colossians 1:13).

9. Remember that the light of God's Word overcomes the devil. *"But everything exposed by the light becomes visible — and everything that is illuminated becomes a light"* (Ephesians 5:13 NIV).

10. Hold on to God's promises. *"Through these he has given us his very great and precious promises, so that through them you may participate in the divine nature, having escaped the corruption in the world caused by evil desires"* (2 Peter 1:4 NIV).

11. Believe that the Lord is exalted above the enemy. *"Yours, O Lord, is the greatness, the power and the glory, the victory and the majesty; for all that is in heaven and in earth is Yours; Yours is the kingdom, O Lord, and You are exalted as head over all"* (1 Chronicles 29:11).

12. Praise God that you are in His kingdom. *"I will give you the keys of the kingdom of heaven, and whatever you bind on earth will be bound in heaven, and whatever you loose on earth will be loosed in heaven"* (Matthew 16:19).

3

Winning Through Resurrection Power

How many times have you ended up in a horrible tangle — all from your own doing? Finally, when the mess looks overwhelming, you cry, "God, HELP!" The good news is that you don't have to wait until you reach the breaking point. God has power for your everyday life — not just for the bad days. It is power that will reassure you that your life is in His total control.

Whatever your current tangle may be, God's power enriches your communion with Christ. Then, when Jesus comes again, that same power will physically resurrect your body into the heavenlies!

God holds special power to do all these things and more. The Old Testament saints glimpsed it, but we have its fullness available to us today. In his letter to the Philippians, Paul revealed the importance of God's power to enrich our lives: *"That I may know Him and the power of His resurrection, and the fellowship of His sufferings, being conformed to His death"* (Philippians 3:10).

Paul was not just casually saying, "Oh, I wish I knew Jesus and what His power was all about." The Greek verb "to know" really means "to know *completely*." I believe that Paul's burning desire was to experience every facet of the Lord's personality in his own life. Why would Paul desire this? Naturally, we all want to be more like Jesus, but the key is that when we know Him this way, His resurrection power divinely transforms our personalities and is evidenced in our lives.

Resurrection Works Miracles

The word "power" in Philippians 3:10 comes from the Greek word *dunamis*, meaning "miracle-working power." God gave Christians two kinds of power. One of these is *exousia*, meaning "authority." Jesus spoke of this kind of authority when He said, *"I give you the authority to trample on serpents and scorpions, and over all the power of the enemy, and nothing shall by any means hurt you"* (Luke 10:19). We have this power of authority in Jesus's name. But the power of resurrection differs from authority. It is *dunamis* — miracle-working power. What does this power achieve for us? The answer is defined in the word "resurrection."

Shadows of Things to Come

Several Old Testament men glimpsed the resurrection power that we now possess. Abraham understood resurrection, although he was not physically resurrected. He knew that if he sacrificed his son Isaac on Mount Moriah, God would raise the child to life from the ashes (Genesis 22:1–19). Elisha laid upon a dead child's body, and the boy came back to life (2 Kings 4:32–37). Ezekiel saw the work of resurrection power when, in a vision, God raised an entire valley of skeletons back to life (Ezekiel 37:1–14).

These three men received glimpses of physical resurrection. But spiritual resurrection must precede physical resurrection, as indicated in Ephesians 2:

> *And you He made alive, who were dead in trespasses and sins . . . But God, who is rich in mercy, because of His great love with which He loved us, even when we were dead in trespasses, made us alive together with Christ (by grace you have been saved), and raised us up together, and made us sit together in the heavenly places in Christ Jesus. (vv. 1, 4–6)*

A sinner cannot receive physical resurrection power without first having spiritual resurrection. He or she must first be spiritually "raised" into heavenly places in Christ Jesus in order to benefit from His power. Once spiritually resurrected, the new believer receives a new life in Christ and, with it, new power for their present and eternal life.

Do you realize that unsaved people are actually dead? God calls them "dead in trespasses" (Ephesians 2:1, 5). Even believers can carry the look of death because sin has deteriorated their physical bodies. But through resurrection power, the erosion of sin can be stopped and even reversed!

When we accept Jesus as our Savior, we can apply His resurrection to everything we do. His power will benefit us now as well as for eternity. Let me add that, as we partake of resurrection power, it radiates and fills the lives of others. Have you ever wondered why the New Testament believers had such effective ministries? They knew how to walk in continual resurrection!

Our Daily Bread

Believers in the early Church found that Communion at the Lord's table filled and overflowed their lives with resurrection power. Today, the bread of Communion should affect us the same way. It should cause us to partake of resurrection.

You can have tremendous knowledge of God's Word, but just possessing such knowledge doesn't make you a partaker of resurrection. If I invited you to share a steak dinner, but you only admired it and said, "It looks delicious," then that steak dinner would fail to bring you sustenance. Likewise, you can know every promise in God's Word — yet still fall short of those promises through a lack of resurrection power.

This must be very grievous to God. He has imparted the power of His Son's fullness to Christians, but many of them still choose defeat. We cannot afford merely to watch life from the sidelines. We must grasp the power that God has given us — a power so vital that it was outlined in the Old Testament.

You may say, "The Old Testament people didn't have Communion." No, but God did provide examples in how they could partake of resurrection power. These examples concern the use of leavened and unleavened bread.

When the Israelites were in bondage to the Egyptians, God told the members of each household to sacrifice a lamb and apply its blood to the doorposts of their houses (Exodus 12:3–7). For us, this application of blood represents our application of Christ's blood to our lives through the new birth.

After applying blood to their doorposts, the Israelites ate the lamb with bitter herbs and unleavened bread (Exodus 12:8). Why did the Israelites eat the bread? Because after the blood had provided them with God's grace and mercy, the bread empowered them with supernatural sustenance for the trials they were about to face.

God promises us more than the application of His Son's blood as a cleansing from sin. The new birth is just that — a new beginning. From that time forward, there will be growing pains: tests and trials. Such trials are our opportunities to taste the daily bread of resurrection and to emerge from them victoriously!

Unleavened Bread

Unleavened bread is pierced before baking so that steam can escape; this keeps the bread from rising. Jesus referred to Himself as the "Bread of heaven" in John 6:50–51. He is our pierced bread. Biblical prophecies foretold the piercing of Jesus's hands and feet on the cross (Psalm 22:16; Zechariah 12:10). John 19:37 said that the men who crucified the Lord "*look*[ed] *on Him whom they pierced.*"

But what happened after Jesus was pierced? He was resurrected! Today, Jesus is our raised — or leavened — bread. Because of His piercing and subsequent resurrection, those who believe in Jesus can also be raised into the miraculous power of His life!

Leavened Bread

If leavened bread is symbolic of rising power, then why did the Old Testament primarily emphasize unleavened bread? No sacrifices were offered with leaven, and before the Feast of Unleavened Bread, leaven was removed from Jewish households (Exodus 12:15). However, I did some further study and discovered two types of Old Testament offerings that required leavened bread. One of the offerings is found in Amos 4:5:

"Offer a sacrifice of thanksgiving with leaven,
Proclaim and announce the freewill offerings;
For this you love,
You children of Israel!"
Says the Lord God.

Leavened — or raised — bread was included in the Old Testament law of peace offerings for thanksgiving (Leviticus 7:13 RSV). Why? The New Testament answers by saying, *"Be anxious for nothing, but in everything by prayer and supplication, with thanksgiving, let your requests be made known to God"* (Philippians 4:6). Thanksgiving is the key ingredient that raises our prayer requests into the presence of God!

The other offering that required leavened bread occurred during the Feast of Weeks (Pentecost). Traditionally, the Israelites offered two raised loaves of bread and waved them before God: *"You shall bring from your dwellings two wave loaves of two-tenths of an ephah. They shall be of fine flour; they shall be baked with leaven. They are the firstfruits to the* LORD" (Leviticus 23:17).

The full significance of offering raised bread at Pentecost was revealed when, after the Lord's resurrection, God poured out His Spirit according to His promise in Acts 1:8: *"But you shall receive power when the Holy Spirit has come upon you; and you shall be witnesses to Me in Jerusalem, and in all Judea and Samaria, and to the end of the earth."* In this verse, the word for "power" is *dunamis* — miracle-working power! Here, the two loaves are a representation of God uniting the Jews and gentiles in one covenant; the two loaves become one people in Him.

Just as the two waved loaves constituted the Old Testament Israelites' firstfruits to the Lord, today we are the firstfruits of salvation through Christ: *"Of His own will He brought us forth by the word of truth, that we might be a kind of firstfruits of His creatures"* (James 1:18). To the Ephesian gentiles, Paul explained how Jesus broke the barrier that once separated them from God: *"But now in Christ Jesus you who once were far off have been brought near by the blood of Christ. For He Himself is our peace, who has made both one, and has broken down the middle wall of separation"* (2:13–14).

40 Years of Miracle Bread

Aside from feasts, offerings, and rituals, bread appears in one other place in the Old Testament. When the Jews ate of this bread, supernatural things happened to them. This bread was the manna that the Israelites ate for 40 years while wandering in the wilderness. Manna lifted them into the shelter of God's divine protection and preservation.

Although we don't know for certain, manna was most likely unleavened since Jesus compares it to the bread of Passover and His own body in John 6:58 (it is also described as being like a "wafer" in Exodus 16:31). It might get tiring to eat the same thing for 40 years, but just think of all that resurrection power! Deuteronomy 29:5 states that not even their sandals and clothes wore out during that entire 40 years (I'd like to have a wardrobe like that!). The benefits of God's supernatural power of preservation were imparted to the Israelites because they partook of the *"bread of heaven"* (Psalm 78:24).

Despite a very difficult situation that was their own fault, God still preserved the Israelites. So it is with resurrection power for us today. Although we may create some disastrous situations, we can rectify those disasters and gain miraculous victories through the resurrection power of Jesus Christ.

The Bread of Life

When you were born again, God gave you enough resurrection power to raise you into the fullness of His kingdom. In Matthew 13:33, Jesus compared God's power to leaven: a small amount contains enough rising power for a large amount of meal: *"The kingdom of heaven is like yeast which a woman took and mixed in sixty pounds of meal until it had leavened the whole batch"* (MEV). Just a small amount will affect the entire batch. Likewise, God has given you enough resurrection power to transform every area of your life. If you look through a concordance of the Bible, you'll find that every New Testament reference to bread speaks of leavened, or raised, bread. Why? Because after Jesus was pierced, He was raised; and through resurrection power, He then raised His people.

Jesus broke raised bread with His disciples at the Last Supper. By faith, Jesus believed that His disciples would be filled with His life. This surprised me because many churches serve small, unleavened wafers at Communion. We should take raised bread because we are partaking of resurrection.

Is your life as flat as a cracker? Tell yourself that you don't want unleavened bread anymore! I want leavened bread that will raise me up. *"This is the bread which comes down from heaven, that one may eat of it and not die"* (John 6:50).

In Matthew 15:21–28, a gentile woman's daughter was suffering from demonic possession. This woman came to Jesus and requested deliverance for her child: *"Have mercy on me, O Lord, Son of David! My daughter is severely demon-possessed"* (v. 22).

However, Jesus did not heal the girl immediately. Instead, He answered, *"I was not sent except to the lost sheep of the house of Israel. . . . It is not good to take the children's bread and throw it to the little dogs"* (vv. 24, 26).

But the woman was very persistent, saying, *"Yes, Lord, yet even the little dogs eat the crumbs which fall from their masters' table"* (v. 27). That is so powerful! Just a crumb of resurrection power can deliver you from any hindrance between you and God. Just a crumb brings your life into all the fullness of Jesus.

Perhaps you say, "Marilyn, you are carrying this to an extreme!" I thought you might say that, so I want to take it even a bit further.

Paul knew how to obtain resurrection power. In Acts 27, one of Paul's journeys on a ship is described. Before leaving port, Paul had advised the ship's crew, "We should winter here because the weather could be stormy." But they didn't listen, and they departed with Paul anyway. Soon, a very dangerous storm hit. Because their lives were in danger, Paul asked the men to fast with him. I thought this was very interesting — a crew of unbelieving men fasted — and it worked! When the storm subsided, Paul broke the fast:

> *While the day was coming on, Paul besought them all to take meat, saying, This day is the fourteenth day that ye have tarried and continued fasting, having taken nothing.*
>
> *Wherefore I pray you to take some meat: for this is for your health: for there shall not an hair fall from the head of any of you.*

And when he had thus spoken, he took bread, and gave thanks to God in presence of them all: and when he had broken it, he began to eat.
(Acts 27:33–35, KJV)

Paul advised the crew, "Take some meat." Why did he himself take bread? Because after his ordeal on the ship, he needed supernatural strength — the resurrection power that united him with Christ. When Jesus broke bread with His disciples, He said, *"This is My body which is broken for you"* (1 Corinthians 11:24). Paul knew that in the breaking of bread came the strength that saved the world. By breaking bread, he received that strength for himself.

The Bread of Health and Strength

In addition to giving us eternal life, raised bread is also intended to infuse our physical bodies with strength. According to Paul, this power even lengthens our lifespans! But if we take the raised bread of the Lord's table without partaking of the power within, the promise works in reverse. *"For he who eats and drinks in an unworthy manner eats and drinks judgment to himself, not discerning the Lord's body. For this reason many are weak and sick among you, and many sleep"* (1 Corinthians 11:29–30).

Paul made a very strong statement here! Because people failed to acknowledge the power that Jesus imparted through raised bread, some were sick and weak, and some even died. Why? Because they ate and drank damnation to themselves by not receiving what God had offered through the ordinance of Communion. It is so important for Christians to stop seeing Communion as merely a one-day ritual! They must receive it as the eternal power it represents to heal and strengthen them and lengthen their lifespans.

When Jesus served Communion to His disciples, He likened the bread to His own body. We are His body; therefore, we can experience His resurrection. Don't just take the blood (salvation); continue in God's power by also taking the bread!

The Bread of Divine Revelation

In addition to giving us health, strength, and long life, resurrection power promises divine revelation, as revealed in Luke 24:13–34, in an incident that occurred after Jesus's resurrection.

After Jesus had been crucified, His disciples were crushed. How could Jesus be king if He had been crucified? It seemed as though their world had fallen apart. Two of them were walking down a path together when suddenly they were joined by another man — the Lord Himself. But the disciples failed to recognize Him. Even when Jesus began encouraging the men with Scriptures, they did not know who He was. How many times do we fail to recognize the Lord because we are wrapped up in our own defeat?

"Come, break bread with us," the two men said to Jesus. He accompanied them to a home, where they broke bread together. When the Lord broke the bread, the men realized, "We have been speaking and communing with the risen Christ!"

As the disciples broke bread with Christ, they finally realized that He was indeed the risen Lord. The bread of Communion is more than just a symbol of the Last Supper. It is an ongoing, dynamic source of revelation and resurrection power! Remember, Paul said we must know Jesus in the power of His resurrection (Philippians 3:10). Once you partake of the ultimate host — Jesus Christ — your life will never be the same.

Strategies for Winning

You may ask, "What is the importance of taking Communion today? It's only bread." Yes, but that bread represents God's power on our behalf! It can quicken our faith to receive healing, strength, long life, and unity in the body of Christ — everything that the broken body of Christ has provided for us. We can even receive revelation knowledge of Jesus and His Word! He has power for every aspect of our daily lives, if only we will receive it.

At the Last Supper, Judas, the Lord's betrayer, ate of the raised bread that Jesus broke. David prophesied of this moment: *"Even my own familiar friend in whom I trusted, **who ate my bread**, has lifted up his heel against me"* (Psalm 41:9, emphasis added). Why the emphasis? The point is, Judas had tasted resurrection power, yet he turned his back on Jesus. This is far worse than just picking at the resurrection bread. Judas was saying, "Raised bread isn't good enough for me." That is why this betrayal weighed so heavily against him.

Anastasis is the Greek word for "resurrection." One of its meanings is "a standing up again." God's miracle power will cause you to stand up to your problems — His way — rather than become entangled in them. No matter what your situation may be, resurrection power makes you a victor over circumstances, mentally, emotionally, physically, and of course, spiritually.

If you are depressed, you need emotional resurrection. If you are sick, you need physical resurrection. Lost souls need spiritual resurrection. Do you have a need? Are you experiencing attacks or trials? Then rejoice, because God has given you resurrection power. His precious resource to lift you above worldly traumas into heavenly places with Christ!

❶ *Don't Be a Picky Eater*

A common reason that Christians fail to receive resurrection power is because they are "picking" at each other. Instead of picking, we should allow the bread of resurrection to unite us in Christ. Having been born into God's family, we celebrate our oneness in Him through Communion. It is a time for rejoicing together. A person who has bitterness in their heart should not take Communion without first repenting of wrong attitudes. Then they can allow resurrection power to restore the breach and bring harmony.

> *The cup of blessing which we bless, is it not the communion of the blood of Christ? The bread which we break, is it not the communion of the body of Christ? For we, though many, are one bread and one body; for we all partake of that one bread.*
> (1 Corinthians 10:16–17)

When we're feasting on the bread of God's resurrection power, we will stop picking at each other. When someone confides in me, "I don't like this speaker" or "I don't agree with that preacher," I automatically think, *Honey, you aren't partaking of resurrection. If you were, you would be praying — not picking.*

Do you feel happy when guests at your dinner table only pick at the food? Of course not. You think that they dislike your cooking. The best guests are those who eat everything in sight. Sometimes, when my family was young, I would return home from traveling, and they would say, "We have been eating frozen food and going to restaurants. We want your cooking!" Those words made me feel so warm inside. When you cook a delicious meal, food is rarely left over. But I wonder how Jesus feels when we "pick" at His resurrection bread? How must He feel when we take Communion without applying its full significance to our lives, or when we pick at each other rather than letting resurrection power bind us together in Him?

I don't always agree with every Bible teacher on every subject, and I guarantee that you won't either. But the important thing is that we are united in a personal way with Christ and, therefore, with other believers. It's time that we stop picking at one another and begin feasting on raised bread!

❷ *Receive the Bread of Unity*

Jesus is our bread that raises us into divine harmony where there once was division. Now all those who believe in Jesus can be united into a covenant with God that was formerly reserved for the Jews. Not only do we have peace with God, but we also have peace with each other. Those believers who can't wait to pick fights with other Christians over points of doctrine aren't partaking of resurrection power.

If you are easily offended by other Christians, then you need resurrection power! When your life is filled with resurrection power, people will no longer offend you. You will be dead to offenses and alive to Jesus. I like to put it this way: dead men don't scream. When resurrection power flows in your life, you will be dead to the world's confusion. Instead of screaming at people, you will love them and pray for them to be raised also.

❸ *Receive the Bread of Power*

Did you know that God started a book about you before your birth? In it, He described your looks, your character — everything about you. Your physical substance may be imperfect, but God has recorded the details in His book. As you are continually fashioned, God continues His book. It contains such masterful detail that Jesus declared, *"The very hairs of your head are all numbered"* (Matthew 10:30).

Parents love their children and keep records of how they change and grow. In return, their love is so precious! One Easter, my son gave me an orchid to express his love. What a special gesture! My thoughts are precious toward him — but I could never count the number of hairs on his head! God's love for us is immeasurable. It spans from before our births into eternity.

> *How precious also are Your thoughts to me, O God!*
> *How great is the sum of them!*

*If I should count them, they would be
　more in number than the sand;
When I awake, I am still with You.*
(Psalm 139:17–18)

"*When I awake*" refers to physical resurrection. Even after death, God continues to keep track of our bodies. Why? So that He can restore them to perfection upon the arrival of His assigned moment of resurrection.

Once, someone told me that we wouldn't need resurrection power in heaven, but Luke 14:15 says, *"Blessed is he who shall eat bread in the kingdom of God!"* Jesus promised that when we are in heaven, He will serve us (Luke 12:37). I think that our first course will be raised bread. Yes, we will partake of His resurrection forever, but the best part is that we can begin today!

Do you have problems, cares, and worries strewn in your path? An old hymn proclaims, "Rise up, O men of God! Have done with lesser things." Did William P. Merrill, who penned these words, know what he was saying? Perhaps. But let's take those words to heart in light of resurrection power through the raised bread of Communion.

Let me conclude with this: Don't settle for less than the resurrection power of Jesus Christ in your life. You aren't fighting a one-person battle. God has given you the ability to attain your goal: knowing Jesus completely through resurrection power. The next time you break Communion bread, be determined to receive the Lord's power for your life: strength, healing, and revelation for your every need! In 1 Corinthians 11:29, Paul said that in order to receive Communion's benefits, we must discern the Lord's body. What does this mean? It means "to distinguish or separate a person or thing from the rest, in effect equivalent to: to prefer, yield to him the preference or honor."

When you begin to understand that special mystery — which the bread in Communion supernaturally contains through Jesus's resurrection power — you will then receive the evidence of being raised into heavenly places with Christ Jesus.

4

Winning Against the Antichrist

Crossroads to War

> *"Now when these things begin to happen, look up and lift up your heads, because your redemption draws near."* (Luke 21:28)

End-time prophecies are being fulfilled every day. Internet outlets and television channels report on wars and rumors of wars, strife, plagues, famines, pestilence, and earthquakes. Reports shout that Christians all over the world are hated, tortured, killed, taken to court, and betrayed by family members. Every night, the news tells us about false prophets who are leading many astray, and people's love waning. Crime and lawlessness abound. Parents are killing their children, and children are killing their parents.

Our world has gone mad! Every day, the devil gains new ground, claiming the hearts and minds of individuals, families, and nations. Despite all of this, I am not afraid. I am encouraged because Jesus told us 2,000 years ago that these things would come to pass in the last days. Each war, famine, plague, and act of lawlessness shows me that God's plan and purpose for this world are being fulfilled exactly as prophesied.

Man's Final Curtain Call?

The entire subject of the end times is shrouded with mystery and centuries of heated theological debate, but no aspect of the end times is as misunderstood as Armageddon. It strikes fear in the hearts of some. However, to others, "Armageddon" has become nothing more than a term signifying the struggle between good and evil; or a bloody war without winners — the end of mankind.

Armageddon will be a terrible battle that creates a river of blood. It is the final rebellion of Satan and man against God. The Antichrist will gather a global army against Israel and ravage the land on the way to Jerusalem, pillaging cities and killing thousands.

However, not once will Satan and his servants lift a weapon against the Lord. When Christ returns with His bride to earth, Satan's army will be destroyed by the voice of our Savior (Joel 2:11). Therefore, there is no real struggle between good and evil because Christ overcomes without lifting a finger.

There will be winners at Armageddon! God's righteous ones — Christians and all the Jews who believe in their Messiah — will receive the title deed to earth. They will live without evil in their midst. They will be part of the divine process of restoring this world to the paradise it was before man's fall from grace.

Armageddon does not mark the end of mankind. In bodies that don't die and with hearts that don't break, mankind will begin an eternity of praise and fellowship with our Father, our Savior, the Holy Spirit, and our brethren in Christ.

A *Story of Restoration*

The entire end-time story is one of restoration and redemption. One of the definitions for "redeem" means "to free by paying a ransom." While we were sinners, we were bound by the penalty of sin. When man sinned, he lost three things:

1. His soul: "*. . . in the day that you eat of it you shall surely die*" (Genesis 2:17).

2. His body: "*. . . For dust you are, and to dust you shall return*" (Genesis 3:19).

3. The earth when it passed into the control of Satan.

Bound to an earth controlled by Satan, we were under the power of evil, but Jesus set us free when He paid the price for our freedom. Through His sacrifice, we were restored to our original master — God — and were again allowed into His blessed arms for a relationship with Him.

Through the events of the tribulation and Armageddon, God gives the world back to its original owner — mankind — and returns it to its original state. Through the rapture of the Church and the return of Jesus Christ, people receive glorified bodies that never again experience sin, pain, hunger, sadness, or death.

The events of the end times bring the story of man's sinfulness full circle, from the beginning, when Adam and Eve sinned, all the way back to His holy embrace.

All Will Be Restored

Praise God that from the very foundation of the earth, He had a plan to restore to us the three things we lost:

1. Our soul: *"Christ has redeemed us from the curse of the law, having become a curse for us"* (Galatians 3:13). When we accepted what Christ did for us on the cross, our souls were redeemed.

2. Our body: *". . . [We] groan within ourselves, eagerly waiting for the adoption, the redemption of our body"* (Romans 8:23). Jesus will give us perfected bodies.

3. The earth: *". . . You were sealed with the Holy Spirit of promise, who is the guarantee of our inheritance until the redemption of the purchased possession, to the praise of His glory"* (Ephesians 1:13–14). Jesus will retrieve the earth from Satan.

The restoration of the earth is a two-fold process that involves both redemption and regeneration. The earth was initially man's property (Genesis 1:26–30). But when man sinned, Satan was able to "purchase" the earth. He possesses the earth now, but I believe God's Word shows that the law of inheritance is greater than that of possession, as indicated by the Jew's return to their nation of Israel. The earth may be Satan's now, but we are the rightful heirs and will hold the title deed to the earth once again.

In the Bible, the difference between an inherited possession and a purchased possession is the type of ownership. An inheritance is permanent; a purchased property is temporary, much like a rental or lease in today's way of thinking.

Leviticus 25:23–28 says an heir to a property may buy his land at any time if he has the money and can prove he is an heir or a relative of the heir. Repurchasing land is a legal transaction in which the kinsman-redeemer who is able and willing to pay the price of redemption, will take the sealed title deed from the man who bought the land and break the seals open. Once opened, the deed is the kinsman's right to evict the purchaser and take possession of the land.

Christ is our kinsman-redeemer. He paid the price to possess the earth, but before He can reclaim the land, He must break open the seals to the title deeds of each. In Revelation 5, Jesus receives the title deed. In chapters 6–8, He breaks the seals. Once the seals are opened, Christ has the right to evict Satan from the earth, which He will do during the battle of Armageddon.

A New Earth

The regeneration of the earth is a different process and is set in motion when Christ breaks the seals on the title deed. As each seal is broken, violent forces will rock the earth with devastating power.

According to the Merriam-Webster Dictionary, the transitive verb "regenerate" means "to restore something back to its original strength or properties." It applies to our soul: ". . . *According to His mercy He saved us, through the washing of regeneration and renewing of the Holy Spirit.*" (Titus 3:5); and the earth: "*Assuredly I say to you, that in the regeneration, when the Son of Man sits on the throne of His glory, you who have followed Me will also sit on twelve thrones, judging the twelve tribes of Israel*" (Matthew 19:28).

During the tribulation, God will cleanse the earth with fire. I believe that the intense heat will cause the glaciers to melt and the oceans and seas to evaporate. We already see that there is melting of our glaciers, but this will be even more intense. A canopy of water will form around the earth, and the great weight of water that is lifted from the earth will cause the planet to go back to its original axis. All of this changes the climate to one that is temperate and warm and the atmosphere to one that protects us from the harmful radiation of the sun and outer space.

Finally, I think that the shifting of the land during the tribulation's many earthquakes will reconfigure the continents. This world will barely be recognizable. In fact, God calls it a "new world." It is the same planet on which we currently live, remade into the perfect paradise that Adam and Eve knew.

Armageddon

The word "Armageddon" only appears once in the Bible:

> *For they are spirits of demons, performing signs, which go out to the kings of the earth and of the whole world, to gather them to the battle of that great day of God Almighty. "Behold, I am coming as a thief. Blessed is he who watches, and keeps his garments, lest he walk naked and they see*

his shame." And they gathered them together to the place called in Hebrew, Armageddon. (Revelation 16:14–16)

The meaning of "Armageddon" in Hebrew simply means the "hill of the rendezvous." I've visited this area countless times. I always find the area awesome as I look down from the ruins of King Solomon's once-magnificent horse stable on the hill of Megiddo into the Jezreel Valley. This valley is fertile and lush, with grapes, barley, and potatoes growing there in abundance. The nation of Israel is fed with these crops. It is a calm place where the morning sunshine chases away the mists of the Kishon River.

Before the Israelis turned this area into the nation's breadbasket in the 1950s, it was primarily a swamp. It is so flat that the Kishon River runs slowly through the valley. The valley used to flood when rain came in the springtime, leaving the land standing in water for several months. But with new flood-control systems, the land is kept clear for farming.

It's hard to believe that this serene setting has been the site of countless battles in history and will be the gathering place for Satan's monstrous army at the end of the tribulation.

Armageddon in History

The Jezreel Valley, about 80 miles northwest of Jerusalem, was the crossroads of two ancient trade routes: one leading from the Mediterranean Sea in the west to the Jordan River Valley in the east; and the other leading from Syria, Phoenicia, and Galilee in the north to the hill country of Judah and the land of Egypt in the south.

This triangular plain is roughly 240 square miles and bordered on the southwest by the Carmel Mountain Range and on the north by the hills of Nazareth. It contains rich farmland because of the soil washed down into it from the mountains of Galilee and the highlands of Samaria. It is also the only east-west valley that divides the mountain ranges of Western Israel.

The valley lies at the entrance to a pass across the Carmel Mountain Range on the main highway between Asia and Africa. It is the key position between the Euphrates and Nile rivers. It was a strategic military site and the scene of numerous ancient battles, many of which were fought by the people of Israel.

The king of Megiddo was one of 31 Canaanite kings whom Joshua and the Israelites conquered in order to take the promised land (Joshua 12:21). The land then became the possession of the tribe of Manasseh, but the people were afraid to drive out the Canaanites who lived there because they had chariots of iron (Joshua 17:12–18).

During the period of the judges, the forces of Deborah and Barak wiped out the army of Sisera on the swampy banks of the Kishon River (Judges 4). The kings of Canaan who fought against Israel for repossession of the land were defeated in Taanach on the river's edge (Judges 5:9).

Ahaziah, king of Judah, was attacked on the way to Gur when he fled Jehu and then died in Megiddo (2 Kings 9:27). All the people associated with King Ahab's reign, including Jezebel, were assassinated by the followers of Jehu in the Valley of Jezreel (2 Kings 9–10). The Philistines were victorious over King Saul there (1 Samuel 31:1–3), and the Egyptians mortally wounded Josiah, king of Judah, when he attempted to intercept the army of Pharoh Necho in the valley (2 Kings 23:29).

The world's final battle, Armageddon, will begin here in this valley, but it won't be fought there. Megiddo is only the gathering place. Once assembled, the Antichrist's demon-powered army will march in absolute precision down the Valley of Jezreel to the Jordan River Valley and head south. They will turn west near Jericho and head to Jerusalem, where the final battle takes place in the Valley of Jehoshaphat (also known as the Kidron Valley).

The End Times

As you study Armageddon and the events leading up to it, it's important to understand that you won't know exactly when the rapture will occur, nor will anyone be able to definitively say who will be the Antichrist.

God told us that humans only *"know in part"* (1 Corinthians 13:9) because prophecy is a mirror we can only see dimly into (1 Corinthians 13:12). Although prophecies seem difficult, when you compare Scripture with Scripture, you can see the details unfolding and the full scope of the prophecy taking shape. Each day, as we come closer to Christ's return, new events are revealed that help us understand the things He has shown to us in prophecies, dreams, and visions (1 Corinthians 13:10).

Prelude to a Battle

The reason the battle of Armageddon will be so devastating is because God's patience will reach the point where He no longer tolerates man's sins. However, even in the midst of the outpouring of His wrath, God will still show incredible grace and mercy to people who turn from their sins and receive Christ as their redeemer (Matthew 24:13).

The Rapture

We see many instances in the Bible where God has protected His people from harm. Christ's work on the cross was the ultimate example of this protection. Jesus paid the price for our sins so we would not die in our iniquity. His blood was shed so ours would not have to flow.

During the tribulation, God will restore this world to its original, pre-curse condition using fires, earthquakes, and floods. These "birthing pains" will cause great torment to the people on the earth. Many will die, while others wish they could die. God does not want His children to experience these horrors. In a tender act of protection, much like a father pulling his child from the dangers of deep water, Jesus will gather us in His arms.

This gathering together to Christ is the rapture. Jesus does not return to Earth to retrieve us. Instead, Christians who are both living and dead will meet Him in the clouds. First Thessalonians 4:17 says, *"Then we who are alive and remain shall be caught up together with them in the clouds to meet the Lord in the air. And thus we shall always be with the Lord."*

The phrase "caught up" in this verse is translated from the Greek word *harpazo*, which means "to seize, carry off by force." This same idea of physical rescue is expressed by Daniel when he prophesied,

> *"At that time Michael shall stand up,*
> *The great prince who stands watch*
> >   *over the sons of your people;*
> *And there shall be a time of trouble,*
> *Such as never was since there was a nation,*
> *Even to that time.*
> *And at that time your people shall be delivered,*
> *Every one who is found written in*
> >   *the book."* (Daniel 12:1)

The word "rapture" does not appear in the Bible. In modern English, the word means "an expression or manifestation of ecstasy or passion." While this English meaning can refer to our being in an eternal state of ecstasy when we are finally with our Lord, the term is actually derived from the Medieval Latin words *rapture* and *raptus,* which mean the "act of carrying off." Thus, our being carried off into heaven is known as "the rapture."

The world will neither see nor hear Christ at the rapture — they won't know anything has happened. Christians will hear the trumpet of God and the shout of Jesus as the first seal of the title deed of earth is opened (1 Thessalonians 4:16; Revelation 6:1–2). All the world will know is that one second we are on earth, standing side by side with our co-workers and friends, and then the next second we will be gone.

The rapture will happen incredibly fast: *"In a moment, in the twinkling of an eye, at the last trumpet. For the trumpet will sound, and the dead will be raised incorruptible, and we shall be changed"* (1 Corinthians 15:52). In this verse, the Greek word for "moment" is *atomos,* which means "indivisible, an atom of time." When something is indivisible, it is so microscopically small that it can't become any smaller. Imagine a measure of time that is so fast it couldn't be any faster — much like the speed of light. The rapture of the church will be even faster.

The world won't be able to see what happens to us, but they will come up with many reasons for our departure, perhaps a mass conspiracy or UFO abduction. Only a few on earth will comprehend what has happened and turn to God as a result.

During the rapture, the dead in Christ will rise first (John 5:25; 1 Corinthians 15:23, 52), and then the living will be physically caught up into the clouds to meet our Lord for the first time. We will then begin our eternal fellowship and worship of Christ (1 Thessalonians 4:16–17).

Who Will Go

Anyone who does not believe in God or that Christ is their Lord and Savior will not go in the rapture. It's important to understand that not every person who calls himself a Christian will be involved in this pre-tribulation rapture.

In Revelation 12:1–6, the rapture is pictured as a woman traveling in childbirth. The baby boy she delivers has the authority *"to rule all nations with a rod of iron. And her Child was caught up to God and His throne"* (v. 5).

I believe the woman is the entire Christian church because she is clothed with the sun and is wearing a crown of 12 stars. The sun shows that she is the light of the world, the 12 stars are the 12 apostles, and the moon under her feet shows that she has the powers of darkness under her (Luke 10:19). The child she delivers is the overcoming church.

Similarly, in Revelation 3, Christ calls the churches by name. The Laodicean church is left behind at the rapture. God "spews" this church out of His mouth because these people do not know Christ (v. 16). They are backsliders and lukewarm Christians who only sit in pews, waiting for services to get over so they can show off their new car, clothes, or jewelry. They neither love nor hate Christ; they are indifferent. When they gather for services, they do not invite Him into their midst. He has to stand at the door of their building and knock (Revelation 3:20).

The overcoming Christians will look like the Philadelphia church. They are Christians who keep God's Word and stand on it in patience and faith. Christ promised them that He would keep them *"from the hour of trial which shall come upon the whole world, to test those who dwell on the earth"* (Revelation 3:10). Jesus will deliver them from the wrath of the tribulation.

Satan will try to keep the church from entering heaven, engaging in battle with the archangel Michael. The dragon will not be able to keep the saints from gathering with Christ. His bitter contest will end with his expulsion from heaven and the end of his reign as "prince of the power of the air" (Ezekiel 28:18; Daniel 8:10–13; Revelation 12:7–10).

In anger, Satan will set out to destroy the remnant church — these are the lukewarm Christians who turn to God after the rapture (Revelation 12:12–17). These new Christians will flee to the mountains, and nature will protect them (Revelation 12:14–16).

The Tribulation

The tribulation will begin after the rapture. This is the final week in Daniel's vision of 70 weeks (Daniel 9:24–27). Daniel said that 70 "weeks" would elapse between the Israelites' return to Jerusalem to rebuild the city and temple and the advent of the Messiah to rule this world. These "weeks" are actually years. This time period is called the Jewish age (the age of law) and will last for 490 years (70 x 7 = 490).

When Jesus came to earth, it was 483 years after the temple was rebuilt. When the Jews rejected Him, the Jewish age was suspended, and the church age (the age of grace) began. the Jewish age resumes when the church is raptured, but only one week remains on the clock. This means the period between the rapture of the church and the second coming of Christ is only seven years.

Daniel described this final week in Daniel 9:27 as a time when the sacrifices and feasts cease and the False Prophet and Antichrist will install his idol, the "abomination of desolation," in the temple (Daniel 12:11).

At the end of the tribulation, which is the end of the Jewish age, the Lord comes back from heaven with His saints and angels *"to finish the transgression, to make an end of sins, to make reconciliation for iniquity, to bring in everlasting righteousness, to seal up vision and prophecy, and to anoint the Most Holy"* (Daniel 9:24). The "reconciliation for iniquity" in this verse is what Jesus was referring to when He said, *"Therefore as the tares are gathered and burned in the fire, so it will be at the end of this age"* (Matthew 13:40). The final judgment of sinners will be at the end of the Jewish age.

Rise of the Antichrist

Before the rapture, the prayers of the saints will have kept evil from completely running rampant on the earth. Christians are the salt that prevents the decay caused by Satan's corruption (Matthew 5:13). When our prayers and authority are taken from the earth, the devil's power will finally blossom into its full force and take shape in the person of the Antichrist.

The powers of the devil are hindered not only by the Holy Spirit but by the body of Christ. Jesus told us that whatever *we* bind on earth will be bound in heaven (Matthew 18:18). We have the authority, and the Holy Spirit partners with our prayers. So it is the church who will hinder the Antichrist from being revealed, and we continue to do so until the moment we are raptured.

I believe the Antichrist is Judas Iscariot returning to earth in an action that counterfeits Jesus's return. I believe this because there is a double prophecy in Psalm 55 that shows both Judas's betrayal of Jesus and the Antichrist's betrayal of Israel, revealing them to be the same man. Also, Judas was more than a man. Jesus called him a devil in John 6:70. The word Jesus used to describe him was *diabolos*, meaning "false accuser, devil, slanderer," which is one of the names of Satan (Revelation 12:10). Judas was the devil incarnate, just as the Lord Jesus was God incarnate. Also, in John 17:12, Jesus calls Judas the "son of perdition," which is the same name Paul uses for the Antichrist in 2 Thessalonians 2:3.

The Antichrist comes from hell and is superhuman. In Revelation 11:7, he is seen coming out of the bottomless pit, which is the abode of lost spirits and wicked dead, the place of their torment (Luke 8:31; Revelation 20:1–3).

He comes from the bottomless pit because Judas was sent there when he died (Acts 1:25).

In fact, the Antichrist's history as Judas Iscariot is revealed in Revelation 17:8, which shows that he was once on earth and then, in John's day, he was not on earth because he was dead. He will ascend out of the bottomless pit and end up in perdition when Jesus casts him into the lake of fire at Armageddon.

Why does the devil want an Antichrist? Satan always wants to emulate everything God does. At one point, the Antichrist will imitate Jesus by dying and coming back to life. That's when the world will follow him and say, "Oh look, he was dead and now he's alive." It's a satanic counterfeit of Christ.

God has a trinity: the Father, the Son, and the Holy Spirit. So, the devil mimics it: Satan, the Antichrist, and the False Prophet. However, unlike the abundant life given through the Holy Trinity, the satanic trinity seeks to steal, kill, and destroy. This is why we need to be awake and aware, recognizing the signs of the Antichrist.

I believe the Antichrist is alive today. Currently, he could very well have some form of influence in a Middle Eastern or European country, but he does not yet hold a prominent position. He will not come to power until immediately after the rapture (Ezekiel 28:12–29; 2 Thessalonians 2:2–7; Revelation 12:9; 13:3–4; 17:8). He will come quietly out of obscurity and quickly gain control (Revelation 13:1). His ascent is fueled by war, which is pictured as the second seal and the red horseman in Revelation 6:3–4.

As you go through the Bible and look for the Antichrist, you will find signs of him from Genesis through Revelation. When Adam and Eve sinned in the garden of Eden, God cursed Satan saying, *"I will put enmity between you and the woman, and between your seed and her Seed; he shall bruise your head, and you shall bruise His heel"* (Genesis 3:15). The seed of the woman is Christ. Satan's "seed" is the Antichrist.

The Antichrist has many names in the Bible — the Beast, the Prince of Tyre, and the Worthless Shepherd are just a few. From Bible prophecy, a portrait of the Antichrist can be painted that will make him easy to recognize for those who have the discernment to see.

Ethnicity and Homeland

Even though he may be living today and have some form of authority, the Antichrist will not come into a prominent position of power until after the rapture of the "overcoming church" (1 Thessalonians 4:13–18; Revelation 3:21).

He will bring destruction. Zechariah prophesied:

*I am raising up **in the land** a shepherd who does not care for those being destroyed, or seek the young or heal the maimed or nourish the healthy, but devours the flesh of the fat ones, tearing off even their hoofs.*

"Woe to my worthless shepherd,
 who deserts the flock!
May the sword strike his arm and his right eye!
Let his arm be wholly withered, his right eye
 utterly blinded!" (Zechariah 11:16–17 ESV, emphasis added)

The Antichrist will be at least part Jewish and born within the boundaries of the ancient Assyrian empire. When prophesying about the end times, Isaiah states:

> *"Woe to Assyria, the rod of My anger*
> *And the staff in whose hand is My indignation.*
> *I will send him against an ungodly nation,*
> *And against the people of My wrath*
> *I will give him charge,*
> *To seize the spoil, to take the prey,*
> *And to tread them down like the mire*
> *of the streets."* (Isaiah 10:5–6)

The ancient Assyrian empire is now made up of Iraq and parts of Iran, Syria, Kuwait, and Turkey. So, if the borders of these countries don't change, we can expect the Antichrist to arise out of one of these nations.

In Revelation 13:1, the Antichrist is the beast pictured with seven heads and 10 horns. Six of the seven heads represent world empires that have conquered Israel in the past: Egypt, Assyria, Babylon, Medo-Persia, Greece, and Rome. The seventh head is the Antichrist himself, who will control Israel during the end times. The 10 horns symbolize the 10 nations lying within the borders of these ancient empires that will fall under the Antichrist's rule (Daniel 7:24).

Coming to Power

The Antichrist will first conquer three countries, which will scare seven others to join his confederacy (Daniel 7:24; Revelation 17:12–17). After he builds his empire, armies, and reputation, the Antichrist will focus his attention on Israel. He will offer his help to make peace with Israel's surrounding nations, and Israel will eagerly enter into a seven-year covenant with him. He will then rebuild the temple (Daniel 9:24–27; 11:22). This and the peace he will forge between Israel and the Arab nations will seem to be such a miracle to the Jews that they will believe he is their messiah (John 5:43). As a result, Israel's connection with God and their spiritual heritage will dry up (Joel 1:10–12).

The world will accept the Antichrist because he is a genius in seven areas: intellect (Ezekiel 28:3; Daniel 8:23), oration (Daniel 7:20; Revelation 13:2), politics (Daniel 11:21; Revelation 17:17), commerce (Ezekiel 26:4–5; Daniel 8:25; 11:38, 43), military and government (Isaiah 14:16–17; Daniel 8:24; Revelation 13:4, 7), and religion (2 Thessalonians 2:4).

His prowess as a government leader will show when he welds together opposing forces and unites conflicting countries. He will create an empire out of the former Roman, Greek, Medo-Persian, and Babylonian empires, which currently cover Europe, the Middle East, North Africa, and parts of Asia. The Antichrist's tight grip on political, economic, and military systems will bring the world under satanic control. Even though he affects the entire world, the Antichrist won't be able to conquer all — only Jesus will rule the entire world. The extent of the Antichrist's complete authority is limited to the area of the old Roman empire around the Mediterranean Sea.

While the Antichrist has the world's attention and the hearts of the Jews, Satan tries to prove the Antichrist is the messiah. In an imitation of Christ, the Antichrist is killed, and because the people refuse to bury him (Isaiah 14:19–20), the world will see him "rise from the dead" (Revelation 13:3).

Satan will give the Antichrist new powers to do deceptive signs and wonders (2 Thessalonians 2:9; Revelation 13:2–7), causing people to revere and worship him (Revelation 13:4). They believe he is God and follow his lead as he persecutes the remnant church (Revelation 13:7–8). This satanic religion is described in Revelation 17:1 as a *"harlot who sits on many waters."* I believe the Antichrist's religious system will rule over many people as the kings of the earth will fornicate with this harlot, and the nations of the earth will be drunk with her wine (Revelation 17:2).

Characteristics

Daniel describes the Antichrist as a *"... Horn which had eyes and a mouth which spoke pompous words"* (Daniel 7:20). He will be a persuasive speaker and draw people through his use of words. If you've ever watched documentaries about World War II or the Holocaust, I'm sure you've noticed what a mouth Hitler had. He was an extremely passionate speaker; you can see the radical craziness. Yet he convinced millions of Germans to follow him. Undoubtedly, Hitler was obsessed, oppressed, and possessed by Satan. The way he spoke, the way he devoured, and the way he led people into such terrible atrocities and genocide are evidence of this.

Daniel 8:23 further characterizes the Antichrist as *"a king of fierce countenance"* (KJV) or *"a fierce-looking king, a master of intrigue"* (NIV). Again, if you look at pictures or video footage of some of the wicked rulers of the world who have now fallen, you can see evil in their eyes. Their wickedness begins to show in their facial features and countenance. So it will also be with the Antichrist — his eyes will betray his evil intentions.

The Antichrist will be intellectually brilliant. The Lord spoke through Ezekiel:

> "Son of man, say to the prince of Tyre,
>   'Thus says the Lord God:
>
> "Because your heart is lifted up,
> And you say, 'I am a god,
> I sit in the seat of gods,
> In the midst of the seas,'
> Yet you are a man, and not a god,
> Though you set your heart as the heart of a god
> (Behold, you are wiser than Daniel!
> There is no secret that can be hidden from you!
> With your wisdom and your understanding
> You have gained riches for yourself,
> And gathered gold and silver into your treasuries;
> By your great wisdom in trade you
>   have increased your riches,
> And your heart is lifted up because of
>   your riches)." (Ezekiel 28:2–5)

According to Isaiah 14:16–17, he will also be a military and governmental mastermind.

> *"Those who see you will gaze at you,*
> *And consider you, saying:*
> *'Is this the man who made the earth tremble,*
> *Who shook kingdoms,*
> *Who made the world as a wilderness*
> *And destroyed its cities,*
> *Who did not open the house of his prisoners?'"*

The Antichrist will have a tight grip on political, economic, and military systems. After building his realm, the Antichrist will raise taxes, especially in Israel, and the pressure on them will be tremendous. Daniel 11:20 tells us, *"There shall arise in his place one who imposes taxes on the glorious kingdom."*

However, he will offer peace to war-weary Israel, and this temporary peace will make him seem like a miracle worker. Israel will accept him as their Messiah, and he will be popular for a period of time. *"For when they say, 'Peace and safety!' then sudden destruction comes upon them, as labor pains upon a pregnant woman. And they shall not escape"* (1 Thessalonians 5:3).

All of this will happen because of the Antichrist's cunning deceit, and deception will prosper during his rule. *"He shall come in peaceably, and seize the kingdom by intrigue*" (Daniel 11:21). Remember, Satan will give him and the False Prophet the power to do counterfeit miracles and people all over the world will begin to revere and worship the Antichrist as god.

> *"The coming of the lawless one is according to the working of Satan, with all power, signs, and lying wonders, and with all unrighteous deception among those who perish, because they did not receive the love of the truth, that they might be saved"* (2 Thessalonians 2:9–10). See also Revelation 19:20.

Once the Antichrist imposes himself in Israel, he will rebuild the temple in Jerusalem, including the holy of holies. The False Prophet will then make a talking idol of the Antichrist and place it in the temple. The Antichrist wants to be worshiped. Remember what caused Satan to fall from heaven? He said, "I want to be like God." He tried to exalt himself above God, and God threw him out (Ezekiel 28:12–19). When his idol is set up in the temple, the Antichrist's allies will become disillusioned with him, and Israel will rebel against him. This will be about three and a half years into the Antichrist's seven-year rule.

"Through his cunning
He shall cause deceit to prosper under his rule;
And he shall exalt himself in his heart.
He shall destroy many in their prosperity.
He shall even rise against the Prince of princes;
But he shall be broken without human means."
(Daniel 8:25)

Satan is the original terrorist, and he is the spirit guiding present-day terrorism. As an agent of Satan, the Antichrist will also be anti-*Christian*. As with Hitler, people will follow him, and they will persecute the "lukewarm" church. During these horrible years, the Bible says many will be deceived and lose their salvation. But after the worst three and a half years of their lives, the saints who remained faithful will be raptured.

To summarize, the Antichrist will:
- Be at least part Jewish and born within the boundaries of ancient Assyria.
- Be a persuasive speaker with a fierce countenance.
- Be intellectually brilliant and a governmental mastermind.

- Have a tight grip on political, economic, and military systems.
- Raise taxes, but bring temporary peace to Israel and the Arab states.
- Rebuild the temple and proclaim himself to be god.
- Persecute the lukewarm church.
- Rule for seven years, but eventually be defeated by Christ and thrown into the lake of fire.

Marching to War

Jesus Claims the Earth

While the Antichrist is luring the world's armies to Armageddon for the final showdown, the scene in heaven is triumphant. In Revelation 10:1–4, we see a mighty angel plant one foot on the earth and the other on the sea. This is not yet Jesus's physical return to earth; it is the figurative move He will make in order to restore the world to its rightful owners — mankind.

When the seventh and final seal is opened, Jesus will fulfill the law of inheritance and prove He is the rightful heir to the world. By setting His feet on the earth,

He legally claims the right to kick the trespasser — the devil — off His property (Psalm 24:1).

In another figurative move, Jesus gives the title deed of the earth to John and instructs him to eat it. This symbolizes mankind's legal inheritance to the earth. By eating it and finding it to be sweet on his lips but bitter in his stomach, John shows that the possession of the world is good, but events that will lead up to this moment cause great sorrow to the human race (Ephesians 1:11–14; Revelation 10:10).

Death of the Two Witnesses

The Antichrist will watch as his empire crumbles, and in his fury, he will attack those who have attacked him — the two witnesses. He kills them in Jerusalem and will leave their bodies lying on the street for three-and-a-half days for the world to see (Revelation 11:7–10).

As people watch these events unfold, they will rejoice at the deaths of the two witnesses, but then be amazed when they see them come back to life and ascend into heaven (Revelation 11:11–12). As the two witnesses are being raptured, an earthquake in Jerusalem will kill 7,000 of its inhabitants (Revelation 11:13).

It's a tipping point. This is when the stage will finally be set for Armageddon.

In the Valley of the Shadow of Death

The fury of the Antichrist will be further kindled by the resurrection and ascension of the two witnesses. They will have made a fool of him, and in retribution, the Antichrist will decide to take his campaign against God and His people to the ultimate level — he will declare war on Israel.

In Revelation 16:16, we see that the Antichrist will gather his armies in Armageddon. Joel 2:2 says this army of the devil will be *"great and strong, the like of whom has never been; nor will there ever be any such after them."*

Joel further compares this multitude to the huge locust swarms of his day (v. 25). Thousands upon thousands of locusts would come over the plains and mountains, blocking out the light of the sun. Their approach could be heard for miles. People knew the locusts came to destroy and that they could do nothing to stop them.

They're Coming!

Likewise, the people will see and hear the coming of the Antichrist's army as they head east out of Armageddon and south down the Jordan River Valley. When they arrive at Jericho, they will turn west toward Jerusalem.

I can imagine people sounding an alarm — perhaps a ram's horn. This horn is called a shofar and was what the Israelites blew before battles in the Old Testament. The shofar makes low, guttural sounds, calling the people to arm themselves and prepare to fight.

As they prepare for the battle of Armageddon, the Israelites will probably have to arm themselves ingeniously. During the former three-and-a-half years, they will have faced natural disasters, demonic attacks, and persecution from the Antichrist. Most likely, only a handful of weapons will remain after all the destruction and confiscation. I believe they will make weapons out of wood and other available materials, creating spears, bows, arrows, and homemade explosives.

They will hear the Antichrist's army as it marches through Israel. The roar of the soldier's feet, their machines, and the sound of their destruction will echo through the air like thunder. The explosions they set off behind themselves will ignite the sky like lightning.

Joel 2:3 says, *"A fire devours before them, and behind them a flame burns."* They are so intent on destruction that the armies of the Antichrist will use bombs and other deadly weapons to turn the land of Israel into a desolate wilderness. Their weaponry will sound and look *"Like the noise of a flaming fire"* (v. 5).

Israel will be set on fire.

The March of Death

Remember, this army will be like no other. There will be no thought of occupying countries or protecting anyone's life or property. The intent of the devil and his soldiers will be to annihilate Israel and God's people. Generals will not weep when their battalions fall due to explosions and radiation. They will push on and keep their eye on the goal of Jerusalem's destruction.

Although it would be easier for the Antichrist to destroy Israel by simply launching a nuclear weapon into the country, I don't believe he'll be able to do this. The massive destruction to the earth caused by the seven seals will destroy most, if not all, of the military's advanced technology, including missile launchers, radar systems, and more. All armies — not just Jerusalem's — will have to use whatever is handy to fight with (Joel 3:10).

I believe that even though the technology is no longer available to launch missiles, the nuclear warheads will still be intact because they will have been protected in subterranean silos. The Antichrist will have the machinery of destruction available but will be forced to bring it to his target on foot.

The Antichrist's army will be extremely agile (Joel 2:4), using horses and maybe tanks and other armored vehicles to help them move with unity and formation through the valleys, mountains, and rough terrain of Israel. They won't break their ranks and will be extremely precise (v. 7). Satan's force will be the most disciplined fighting machine the world has ever witnessed.

Joel 2:8 says, *"They do not crowd each other, they march everyone in his path"* (NASB), meaning they are extremely well-trained. This will be no hodge-podge attack. It will be organized and well-coordinated. Every man will march in unison with the others, and no one will seek attention or praise. They will have a common goal and present a united front against God.

This same verse goes on to say, *"When they burst through the defenses, they do not break ranks"* (NASB). The Antichrist's army will be so well-coordinated that they march forward as one person — nothing will be able to stop them. As part of the devil's plan to torture God's people, they will rape, pillage, and ultimately destroy the villages and towns of Israel on their way to Jerusalem. We saw a glimpse of this on October 7th, 2023, the largest loss of Jewish life since WWII, when Hamas invaded Israel with no other goal but to kill, steal, and destroy.

The Attack

When the armies finally arrive in Jerusalem, they will attack ruthlessly. The soldiers will rush the city and climb the walls, beginning the work of war. Joel 2:9 says, *"They rush on the city, they run on the wall; they climb into the houses, they enter through the windows like a thief"* (NASB). They will ransack, rob, plunder, and strip the houses bare. They will rape the women and take half the people into captivity (Zechariah 14:2).

As you can imagine, the people in Jerusalem will react with fear and horror. They will be in tremendous pain and anguish, turning pale with fright as they realize the enormity of the army that has come to attack them.

Multitudes in the Valley of Decision

When the soldiers are through looting and attacking, they will leave the city and gather in the Valley of Jehoshaphat. This valley is part of the Kidron Valley on the east side of the city, between the temple and the Mount of Olives. I believe this is when the Antichrist will prepare his nuclear weapon and the troops will assemble to leave the area so he can detonate the device.

Although the army will think they are following the commands of their demon-general, they will actually be following God's plan, which calls the army into the Valley of Jehoshaphat in order to judge them (Joel 3:12). The name Jehoshaphat means "Jehovah judged." When they get into the valley, everything will become pitch black. God will darken the sun and moon and stop the stars from shining for 24 hours (Joel 3:15; Zechariah 14:6). It will be as if time stands still. Their machinery will not work, and they won't be able to see so they can march or walk. Every soldier will be forced to remain where he stands.

God calls the Valley of Jehoshaphat the "valley of decision" in Joel 3:14 because, during the 24 hours of inactivity and calm, God will give the nations of the earth one final opportunity to repent of their sins. It will be His final wake-up call to their spirits (v. 12).

Throughout time, God has always shown people His character. He has revealed His glory through nature, the stars, the miracles of life, His Word, and His people. During the tribulation, He will send angels to witness. There will also be 144,000 people who tell His story

(Revelation 14:1), the two witnesses with the power to work miracles (Revelation 11:3), and all of the supernatural judgments. Even after all of that, God will still give the people who reject Him and rebel against His love and authority one more opportunity to change their minds. He will even give them the peace and quiet they need to think clearly about their situation, because God will not send His judgment on anyone until He has first shown mercy.

During these same 24 hours, God will deal with the people who remain in Jerusalem. Many will still be alive, but they will be bleeding, beaten, and frightened. When the darkness descends, I believe they will wonder what kind of trouble has befallen them again, but will then hear the Lord speak to them according to Joel 2:12–13:

> *"Now, therefore,"* says the LORD,
> *"Turn to Me with all your heart,*
> *With fasting, with weeping, and with mourning."*
> *So rend your heart, and not your garments;*
> *Return to the LORD your God,*
> *For He is gracious and merciful,*
> *Slow to anger, and of great kindness;*
> *And He relents from doing harm.*

Repent!

This call to repentance is very beautiful and so typical of God. For centuries, the Jews rejected Him in so many ways. At the very beginning of their nation, they worshiped the golden calf and then the brazen idols and hateful gods of heathen nations. Even though they had received the most powerful demonstrations of God's love and mercy, they still doubted and refused His presence.

They rejected their true Messiah — Jesus. But they will end up accepting a heinous lie of the devil — the Antichrist — as their savior. In choosing Satan's lies of physical peace and prosperity, they show God that His promise of inner peace and soul prosperity isn't good enough. Through it all, however, God's anger against them was and will be slow to boil. His every step, judgment, and sign through the ages was and will be given to show them the truth of who He is and who they are in Him. He has never given up on them, returning time and again to purchase them from the pit of their sins.

God's final attempt to get the Jews' attention will be very loving. He will speak to them in the darkness and tell them, "Today is the day of your salvation." Their situation could not be worse, but in the midst of it all,

God will talk to them, wooing them into the safety of His arms (Joel 2:12–27).

God will want them to give Him their hearts and show repentance through fasting, weeping, and praying. They will not be able to truly repent and accept the Lord's sacrifice without some sort of outward evidence of their changed natures. Even if they don't show their emotions, He will want them to break their hearts in repentance. People who only make an outward show of tearing their garments won't be saved. God will choose those who break their hearts in true repentance (Joel 2:12–17).

Sometimes, people go through the motions of repenting but don't mean it. An example is the story of Cain and Abel. Both offered sacrifices for their sins, but Abel gave with a broken heart and Cain gave, not out of real emotion but as an act of religious responsibility. For that reason, God accepted Abel's sacrifice of repentance but rejected Cain's.

It is interesting to look at the word "repentance" and its various meanings. In Matthew 4:17, when Jesus told the people to *"Repent, for the kingdom of heaven is at hand,"* the root Greek word *metanoeo* was used. Metanoeo means "to think differently." Jesus was calling people to change their lives by changing their minds or attitudes — this is true repentance.

However, in Matthew 27:3, when Judas *"repented himself"* (KJV) after betraying Christ, he only had a change in emotion. The root Greek word here is *metamellomai*, which means "to care afterwards." Judas was remorseful, but he didn't change his heart or his life. This is repentance in name only.

When the Jews repent at the battle of Armageddon, God will promise to be gracious and merciful to them. He will forgive them for their sins and protect them — offering the solution to this and every problem they have. In this time of distress, God will help them because they turn to Him and ask for help. When the Jews accept God's call and ask for His help, they will blow the trumpet, sanctify a fast, and call a solemn assembly. The priests will weep to the Lord in intercession for the people. They will accept Jesus's sacrifice and beg Him to return quickly (Joel 2:15–17).

The Marriage Supper

While all this is happening on earth, a great event is unfolding in heaven: the Marriage Supper of the Lamb. The saints and angels will gather to witness this event.

The Bride of Christ — all the believers who awaited His first coming, who accepted Him after His death and resurrection, and those who asked Him into their hearts during the tribulation — are arrayed in the linen of righteousness, washed clean and white by the blood of the Lamb.

Jesus, revealed as the glorious Christ will appear on a white horse, with His eyes as flames of fire and crowns on His head. His clothes will be dipped in blood. The ceremony is a call to war, and when it is finished, His saints will mount white horses and follow Him (Revelation 19:7–14).

Christ's Return

God will respond to the trumpet call of His people in Jerusalem, and He will order the seventh trumpet to be blown in heaven. With a *"roar from Zion"* (Joel 3:16), Jesus will return with His army — His bride.

The army of the Antichrist will not turn to Jesus while in the valley of decision. Their choice is judged by God, and they will be sentenced to death and eternal damnation. Jesus's war cry (the Word of God) will become the sword of the Lord and slay the Antichrist's army (Revelation 19:13–15). Their blood will flow in a river

200 miles long and four feet deep (Revelation 14:20). I believe this river of blood will flow in the Jordan River Valley, which is 200 miles long from the Sea of Galilee to the southernmost tip of Israel.

This battle will be the harvest in which Jesus separates the wheat from the chaff (Matthew 3:12). The chaff will blow away to the place of unquenchable fire, but the wheat will remain and become the bread that blesses the earth during the millennium.

Nature will respond to Christ's return with lightening, thunder, 60-pound hail, and an earthquake that shakes the world (Jeremiah 10:10; Matthew 24:29-31; Luke 21:25-27; Revelation 11:15-19; 16:17-21). Islands and mountains will move, and entire cities and nations will be destroyed — including Egypt and Edom (Joel 3:19). Babylon will fall in a day. No one will survive and no one will ever live in the city again (Isaiah 13:20-21; Revelation 18:6-8). This leads me to believe that the bomb intended for Jerusalem will instead level Babylon.

This destruction of Babylon will also be the judgment of cults, false religions, and idolatry — all of which are pictured as harlots in Revelation 17. With the return of Christ, the nations will realize the harlot's deception and destroy her once and for all (Revelation 17:16-17).

Jerusalem

Jerusalem will change dramatically at the second coming. When Jesus's feet touch the Mount of Olives, the mountain will rip in two all the way from the Mediterranean Sea to the Dead Sea, which is 1,200 feet below sea level. The waters of the Mediterranean will rush into the Dead Sea, carrying with it many of the soldiers whose bodies will be scattered over the countryside. This new river will flow from Jerusalem (Zechariah 14:4, 8), which has been divided into three parts (Revelation 16:19).

Flesh-eating birds, which will be invited to the Supper of the Great God by an angel, will feast on the bodies of the soldiers (Revelation 19:17–18). The smell of decaying flesh will saturate the air (Joel 2:20).

One of the best outcomes of the battle of Armageddon is that the Antichrist and False Prophet will be thrown into the lake of fire to be persecuted forever. Satan will be chained in the bottomless pit for 1,000 years, and his demons will be expelled from the earth (Isaiah 24:21–22; Matthew 13:41–43; 25:41; Revelation 19:20–21; 20:13).

Christ will take possession of the earth and will walk in victory through the eastern gate of His capital city, Jerusalem. His 1,000-year reign of the world will then begin.

The Aftermath

"It is done!" (Revelation 16:17). When the smoke clears and the rumblings of the earth are silenced, the redeemed in Jerusalem will look out of their walled city to see the countryside of Israel covered with the bodies of soldiers and horses — hundreds of thousands of them — while vultures circle and land on the bodies (Ezekiel 39:4–5, 17–20).

All the people of Israel and the travelers who pass through the land will spend seven months burying the dead. The valley where they bury the Antichrist's army — just east of the Mediterranean Sea — will be named the Valley of Hamon Gog, which means "the company of god," referring to the Antichrist (Ezekiel 39:11–16). People will go through the land, gathering their own weapons and those of the Antichrist's fallen army to use as fuel for their stoves and fireplaces. They will use spears, weapons, and ammunition in place of wood, allowing the earth to recover and replenish itself after the seven years of destruction during the tribulation (Ezekiel 29:9–10).

Men and women will no longer look to the works of their hands or the beauty of their world to bring them contentment or joy; they will no longer be in control. Because of the state of the world, they will be completely reliant on God. The plagues, earthquakes, hail, and fire will have destroyed man's churches, temples, mosques, and altars. His buildings, paintings, sculptures, and other creations will have been obliterated. The places men used to go to experience nature's beauty are gone. The earth will be smoking, boiling, and in ruins. Under Christ's supervision and with the saint's help, the people of the earth will begin the reconstruction of their homes. They will cleanse the earth of the dead, plant their fields, and clothe their bodies.

The Restoration

Many people have incorrectly taught that the millennium is a perfect time on this earth when humans will receive glorified bodies, renewed minds, and nature will be redeemed from its curse. I don't believe this is quite right because the millennium will be a time for perfecting this world and its inhabitants, not for living in perfection. The only people who live in glorified bodies will be the saints who were raptured or resurrected before or during the tribulation.

The Word says that during the millennium, bodies will need to be buried, things will stink, people will need to find ways to keep warm, and employment will be necessary (Ezekiel 39:11–14).

The laws of nature will remain somewhat unchanged because, while the world carries some old curses, new blessings will begin to take shape. Living waters will spring from the house of the Lord — the temple. This river will flow south out of Jerusalem until it breaks into two branches, one that travels to the Mediterranean Sea and the other to the Dead Sea (Ezekiel 47:1; Joel 3:18; Zechariah 14:4, 8).

Everywhere these waters flow, healing will take place. The rivers will bring life to the desert and fresh water to a thirsty people and earth (Isaiah 35:1–2; Ezekiel 47:9). The Dead Sea will be brought to life, allowing a great multitude of fish to thrive in waters that were once so thick with minerals and salt that nothing could live there (Ezekiel 47:8–10). For the first time in history, the Dead Sea will be a living sea. The entire physical nature of Israel will be transformed into a land of abundance and growth.

Things will change slowly during the millennium, but eventually the curse that is on the earth will lessen so that deserts blossom and fields will yield incredible harvests (Isaiah 35:1–2; Joel 2:22; 3:18; Amos 9:13–15).

The heavens will also change. The moon will become as bright as the sun, and the sun's light will increase sevenfold. However, even the stars will reveal that nature is not the source of life. It is God alone who is the source because the light of the Lord and the glory of God will give us the light by which we will see, work, and play (Isaiah 2:4; 11:6–8).

Mankind

Human nature will not fall in line with God's plan as easily as nature does. People will still rebel against Christ, but His salvation will be available to redeem those who continue to sin.

Many people who survive the tribulation and the battle of Armageddon will be unbelievers. However, when Satan is bound, he will no longer be able to deceive (Revelation 20:3). People's eyes will be opened to receive a unique and startling revelation of God's character and glory (Isaiah 11:9; Ezekiel 43:2). I believe that during this time, most people will change their hearts and give their lives to Jesus (Zechariah 8:23), but some people will continue to deny Christ and live in sin.

Everyone living during the millenium will be blessed because the devil is bound, but they will still have to make the choice to follow God and obey His Word. There is a saying, "The devil made me do it;" but although the devil deceives and tries to destroy us, Satan doesn't *make* us do anything. We make the choice to rebel against God and reject His Word. Likewise, people living during the millenium will make the choice to sin, but without the luxury of saying, "The devil made me do it," because he won't be around to lead anyone into temptation.

During the millennium, Christians will receive the tremendous blessing of salvation in its fullest form. Jesus will give us the complete manifestation of inner peace, love, righteousness, and physical healing (Isaiah 9:7; 11:5; 32:1–3; 33:24; 35:5–6; Ezekiel 36:25–26). Long life will also be restored to all people. Isaiah 65:20 says that a child will become an adult at the age of 100. Lifespans will probably reach 900–1,000 years. However, death will not be eradicated.

The population of the earth will have drastically diminished during the tribulation and the battle of Armageddon, but during the millennium, it will increase rapidly. This baby boom proves that people will still fall in love, get married, and raise families during the millennium in the way God planned when He created man (Genesis 1:28, Isaiah 65:17–25).

The Reign of Christ

The first thing Jesus will do when He sets up His earthly kingdom will be to assemble the people together. His angels will gather them from earth and heaven so He can sanctify this incredible congregation of flesh-and-blood humans and glorified saints as they enter into the millennium with Him.

The saints (who will have arrived with Christ on white horses and received glorified bodies and minds when they were raptured or resurrected) will reign with Jesus as kings and priests and help Him guide the nations, bringing a perfect form of government to the world (Revelation 20:4). God will head this world government through Jesus (Daniel 7:13–14), who reigns over the world from the temple in Jerusalem (Isaiah 2:2–4; Zechariah 6:12–13). God's purpose through this government will be to restore a righteous and eternal government on earth as He originally planned (Isaiah 9:6–7; 11:1–9; 42:1–5; Daniel 2:44–45; Luke 1:32–33; Revelation 11:15; 20:4–6; 22:4–5).

King David, in his glorified body, will rule over all Israel under Christ (Ezekiel 37:24–28), and the 12 disciples will rule over one tribe each (Matthew 19:28). The Jews who were redeemed during the battle of Armageddon will become the head of all nations under the Messiah (Deuteronomy 15:6).

During this thousand-year period, God will restore the years that the locust ate, giving the Jews all the land and blessings He promised to Abraham, Isaac, Jacob, and David (Genesis 13:14; Isaiah 60:21; Joel 2:25). Israel will receive all the land east of the Mediterranean Sea and the Nile River and west of the Euphrates River. Generally speaking, the new Israel will cover the land that is now Egypt, Sudan, Ethiopia, Somalia, Saudi Arabia, Oman, the United Arab Emirates, Kuwait, Iraq, Syria, Turkey, Jordan, and Israel.

The gentiles will receive land according to God's plan (Deuteronomy 32:8; Acts 17:26), and all nations will be required to send representatives to Jerusalem once a year to acknowledge Christ at the Feast of Tabernacles (Zechariah 14:16–19; Isaiah 2:1–4). The countries that are not represented at the feast will be cursed with a plague and drought.

The Levitical priesthood will be reestablished and will serve in the millennial temple (Acts 15:13–18). They will perform all the previous offerings, feasts, and rituals of the temple as a form of worship and to show Christ's redeeming work through the pictures of the rituals (Ezekiel 43:19–27; Isaiah 66:19–24). It will be similar to us taking Communion today. Justice and prosperity will fill the earth (Isaiah 29:17; Jeremiah 31:27–28).

The Rain of the Holy Spirit

> *Be glad then, you children of Zion,*
> *And rejoice in the* LORD *your God;*
> *For He has given you the former rain faithfully,*
> *And He will cause the rain to come down for you —*
> *The former rain,*
> *And the latter rain in the first month.* (Joel 2:23)

Something that I consider extremely exciting is when the millennium begins, the Holy Spirit will be poured out on all flesh with tremendous power (Joel 2:28–29). Joel refers to this outpouring of the Holy Spirit as the former and latter rains. He uses this description because Israel's economy and society were primarily based on agriculture, and the former and latter rains had to do with harvest times.

The former rain was the moderate spring rain that came right at planting time to give the seeds moisture to germinate and grow. The latter rains came in the fall in large amounts to make the vegetables and fruit multiply and grow large. Together, these combinations of rain made a bountiful harvest that blessed people throughout the year.

The spiritual meaning of this passage has to do with the glory of the Lord in the Old and New Testaments. The former rain is God's Spirit poured out in the Old Testament, and the latter rain is His glory in the New Testament. We are living in the latter rain, which began on the day of Pentecost. This "rain" is poured out upon us so we can reap a bountiful harvest of souls.

At the beginning of the millennium, something unique and wonderful will happen when the latter and former rains come together and pour out upon all people, showering everyone with the glory of the Lord as He was, is, and will be.

The saints of the Old and New Testaments will enter the millennial reign of the Lord together. They will experience the glory that was revealed to Abraham, shone on Moses's face, guided and protected the Israelites by the pillar of fire and the cloud, and filled the wilderness tabernacle and the temple. They will feel the power manifested on the day of Pentecost that has been pouring out since. This is very exciting to me! I love the way the Holy Spirit moves on people today. It's hard to imagine how much better it will get. The presence of the Lord will truly be incredible during the millennium.

Satan Unleashed

At the end of the thousand years, Satan will be unleashed and allowed to roam the earth, gathering the sinners and rebels who remain. Satan's fury will have only grown during the millennium, and he will set out to finish what he started at the battle of Armageddon. His army will reach Jerusalem, but before anything can happen, fire will come down from heaven and devour the soldiers. God will then throw Satan into the lake of fire, where he will spend eternity in pain and torment (Revelation 20:7–10).

Judgment Day

With Satan and the people who denied Christ cast off the earth, God will begin His final judgment of mankind. All the people who denied Christ will be resurrected from the dead in order to stand before God's great white throne.

God will look in the Lamb's Book of Life to find the name of each person who will stand before Him. This book contains only the names of Christ's followers. Those who are not found in the book are judged for the things they did in life — based upon that which is written in the Book of Works — and then are thrown into the lake of fire (Revelation 20:5, 11–15). Finally, death and hell will be cast into the lake of fire and will never darken the face of earth again (Revelation 20:14).

The saints will not participate in the great white throne judgment because they have already received eternal life. Only the wicked and unsaved dead will participate (Revelation 20:6). Christians will *"all appear before the judgment seat of Christ, that each one may receive the things done in the body, according to what he has done, whether good or bad"* (2 Corinthians 5:10). However, we will not be judged for our iniquities, only our good works so that we can receive rewards.

All Things New

> "For behold, I create new heavens and a new earth;
> And the former shall not be
>   remembered or come to mind.
> But be glad and rejoice forever in what I create;
> For behold, I create Jerusalem as a rejoicing,
> And her people a joy.
> I will rejoice in Jerusalem,
> And joy in My people;
> The voice of weeping shall no
>   longer be heard in her,
> Nor the voice of crying." (Isaiah 65:17–19)

Now I saw a new heaven and a new earth, for the first heaven and the first earth had passed away. Also there was no more sea. Then I, John, saw the holy city, New Jerusalem, coming down out of heaven from God, prepared as a bride adorned for her husband. And I heard a loud voice from heaven saying, "Behold, the tabernacle of God is with men, and He will dwell with them, and they shall be His people. God Himself will be with them and be their God. And God will wipe away every tear from their *eyes; there shall be no more death, nor sorrow, nor crying. There shall be no more pain, for the former things have passed away." Then He who sat on the throne said, "Behold, I make all things new." And He said to me, "Write, for these words are true and faithful."* (Revelation 21:1–5)

When the devil, his demons, followers, and all the bodies of the wicked have been removed from the land and seas, the curse and wages of sin will finally be lifted from humankind and the earth.

God will dwell with men and women on the earth where there will be no more tears, death, sorrow, curses, crying, pain, or night. Sin and death will be gone. The whole plan of redemption will be complete (Revelation 21:4; 22:3–5).

The new heaven and earth will not be a result of an unrecorded catastrophe that occurs after the judgment of the great white throne. They will be the result of the process of restoration and regeneration that started with the tribulation and was completed by Christ during the millennium. It is not possible for Christ to fail, so to say that God destroys the world and creates a new one, even after Christ redeems it, is wrong.

Revelation 21:1 says, *"Now I saw a new heaven and a new earth, for the first heaven and the first earth had passed away. Also there was no more sea."* The Greek word for "passed away" is the same word that is used in 2 Corinthians 5:17 when Paul states, *"If anyone is in Christ, he is a new creation; old things have passed away; behold, all things have become new."* Therefore, Revelation 21:1 doesn't suggest destruction; it is a redemption expression that means former things are passed away. Why would trees applaud and mountains and hills break into song unless they had not once known the weight of the curse of sin and death and then felt that incredible burden lift?

> *"For you shall go out with joy,*
> *And be led out with peace;*
> *The mountains and the hills*
> *Shall break forth into singing before you,*
> *And all the trees of the field shall clap their hands.*
> *Instead of the thorn shall come up the cypress tree,*
> *And instead of the brier shall come*
>   *up the myrtle tree;*
> *And it shall be to the* Lord *for a name,*
> *For an everlasting sign that shall not*
>   *be cut off."* (Isaiah 55:12–13)

This new world will be one of joy and godly substance, not a new creation. It will be a world where there are no more thorns or thistles, no locusts, plagues, blight, mildew, or weeds.

The New Jerusalem

Revelation 21 and 22 describe the New Jerusalem, which comes down from God out of heaven, casting down the glory of God over the world and giving it light. The city has a great wall with 12 gates of pearls. It is made of gold, with walls of jasper, decorations of precious stones, and streets of gold.

The River of Life will flow from the thrones of God and Christ, and the tree of life, which was in the garden of Eden, will stand in the midst of the street on either side of the river. It will yield fruit every month, and its leaves will heal the nations.

Holy Jerusalem will be the home of the bride — the saints whose names are written in the Lamb's Book of Life. The saints will come to live here after the millennium in order to fulfill the promise Jesus gave in John 14:2, *"In My Father's house are many mansions; if it were not so, I would have told you. I go to prepare a place for you."* Jerusalem will be the capital of the universe because

God's throne will be in it. Its citizens will be the kings and priests who dispense the benefits of the water of life and the leaves of the tree of life to the world.

From the creation of the world to its restoration, God has shown us that He loves us and wants us to accept His salvation. He doesn't want us to change, but to accept the love and redemption from Christ that will change us. We are powerless to make ourselves sinless, perfect, and holy. Only Christ in His redemptive Word can accomplish this. What a wonderful message of hope, salvation, and redemption God has given us!

Strategies for Winning

Do you know where you fit into God's plan for this earth? Will you be part of the overcoming church that is raptured before the tribulation? Or are you a Christian in name only? I urge you to search your heart and see if you have truly asked Christ to be the Lord and master of your life.

This message of the end times is meant to inform and inspire you. To help you understand biblical prophecy and to prepare you and your loved ones for events that I believe will happen soon. I also want this book to encourage you as a Christian. When you understand the end times, you understand how perfect God's plan and purpose are for this world and His people. The wicked may rule and reign now, but that will come to an end because God's purpose for the tribulation, Armageddon, and the millennium is redemption and regeneration for the world and mankind.

These events may seem too hard to imagine, but they are only extreme versions of what is going on in a person's life before Christ. Because of original sin, your life without Christ is a perfect battleground for Satan. It is in the same condition as the world is in at the present time — overrun and controlled by wickedness.

Have you experienced tribulations in your life? Have you gone through famine, battles, physical suffering, or natural disasters as the result of your sin, someone else's sin, or sin in the world around you? These tribulations are difficult to live through, but the Holy Spirit is always there to woo you into God's arms.

When Jesus is not the Lord and master of your life, the forces of evil will converge on your soul (mind, will, and emotions) with the ultimate goal of conquering and destroying your spirit. Through it all, God calls you to repent. When you do, Christ comes into your heart and breaks it open. As Christ rules and reigns over your life from the "temple" in your heart, a river of life begins to flow out of your spirit — giving nourishment and new life to your body and soul.

The enemy is defeated in your life, but it can still take a while for things to be restored, healed, and regenerated in your soul and body. You are governed by the Holy Spirit, who repairs what sin has broken — your body and soul.

It's important to remember that God gives you time to change. If He gives this planet 1,000 years to become perfect, then you know that He gives you — His blessed child whom He bought with a tremendous price — time to change and become whole. When you make mistakes, don't condemn yourself; just return to Christ and ask for help and guidance. In the end, you will become a new person whose life shines the light of God on others and whose spirit bears fruit in remarkable ways.

❶ *Wake Up*

Sometimes, I think Christians get overly busy trying to make a living and "just get by." What we need to do is wake up and see what's going on around us. We need to be aware of the spiritual climate we are in and learn how to pray and live during these days. Proverbs 30:8 says, *"Feed me with the food that is needful for me"* (AMPC). I believe we are living in the end times, and we need to know what God's Word says for the days in which we live.

If we read Matthew 24 and the book of Revelation, we'll see that the Antichrist could be alive at this very moment; this is not the time for us to sleep! If we look at people who slept at the wrong time in the Bible, we'd first have to look at Samson. He fell asleep on Delilah's lap, and she proceeded to cut off his hair. He lost his power, his anointing, and his call (Judges 16). Eli, the high priest, was sleeping when God spoke to Samuel. God was moving in a supernatural way in the tabernacle, and Eli was asleep (1 Samuel 3). In Genesis 28, Jacob had a dream that angels were ascending and descending a ladder that reached from earth to heaven. Upon waking, Jacob said, *"Surely the* L<small>ORD</small> *is in this place, and I did not know it"* (v. 16). We must wake up and be aware of God's timing and presence.

In the New Testament, there's an account in Acts 20 when Paul is preaching and a young man is sitting on the third-floor windowsill. He fell asleep and ended up falling out the window, to his death (Paul raised the young man back to life). Now is not the time to fall asleep and backslide. We need to hang on, know what the enemy is doing, and be aggressive in our faith! First Peter 5:8 exhorts us to *"be sober, be vigilant; because your adversary the devil walks about like a roaring lion, seeking whom he may devour."*

❷ Draw Near to God

Now is also not the time to be lukewarm. It is time to draw near to God. If you do, He has a wonderful promise for you:

> *Therefore submit to God. Resist the devil and he will flee from you. Draw near to God and He will draw near to you. Cleanse your hands, you sinners; and purify your hearts, you double-minded. Lament and mourn and weep! Let your laughter be turned to mourning and your joy to gloom. Humble yourselves in the sight of the Lord, and **He will lift you up**.* (James 4:7–10, emphasis added)

In his commentary on the Bible, Matthew Henry expounds beautifully on James 4:10, saying:

> If we be truly penitent and humble . . . we shall in a little time know the advantages of his favour; he will lift us up out of trouble, or he will lift us up in our spirits and comfort us under trouble. The highest honour in heaven will be the reward of the greatest humility on earth.

❸ Have Discernment

Many years ago, when communism was at its height in Russia, Romania, and Eastern Europe, there was a man named Richard Wurmbrand. He and his wife were Jewish and became Christians in Romania during this time. Nicolae Ceaușescu was the communist dictator in Romania, and he was an evil leader who did awful things to his citizens, including the intense persecution of Christians. Richard was put in prison and terribly beaten.

Because this was happening behind the "Iron Curtain," no one knew the extent of the atrocities occurring in communist countries. Eventually, Richard got out and came to America. He came and spoke at our church, and he also testified before Congress. Eventually, he started a ministry called *Voice of the Martyrs*, which exposes the persecution of Christians around the world. Sometimes, it's quite shocking to find out how people are suffering. Why are people suffering and being persecuted? It's the spirit of the Antichrist. First John 4:1–6 states:

> *Beloved, do not believe every spirit, but test the spirits, whether they are of God; because many false prophets have gone out into the world. By this you know the Spirit of God: Every spirit that confesses that Jesus Christ has come in the flesh is of God, and every spirit that does not confess that Jesus Christ has come in the flesh is not of God.*

And this is the spirit of the Antichrist, which you have heard was coming, and is now already in the world.

You are of God, little children, and have overcome them, because He who is in you is greater than he who is in the world. They are of the world. Therefore they speak as of the world, and the world hears them. We are of God. He who knows God hears us; he who is not of God does not hear us. By this we know the spirit of truth and the spirit of error. (Emphasis added.)

John 10:10 tells us that Satan is our enemy, and he is a thief who comes to steal, kill, and destroy; but that Jesus came to give us abundant life. John 3:16 says that God loves the world. The spirit of the Antichrist is against anything God wants to do. Although we often think of the Antichrist in terms of how he will persecute Christians, and he will, there are other, more subversive, tactics he will use. One of which is the perversion of truth.

Some time ago, I saw a woman being interviewed on CNN, and she said, "I'm a Christian, and I believe God wants us to enjoy life. If it feels good, you can do it." I'm sure you have heard similar things from people. That is an antichrist spirit. God is love (1 John 4:8), but He loves us enough to change and transform us, to keep us from doing things that will end up hurting us and those around us. He loves us enough to send Jesus to die for our sins so that we don't go to hell. Therefore, have discernment so you can tell when a deceptive spirit is active. Step four will help you with this.

④ Lean on the Holy Spirit

Depending on the Holy Spirit is so important during these last days. The apostle Paul encouraged the church in Rome:

> *I consider that the sufferings of this present time are not worthy to be compared with the glory which shall be revealed in us. For the earnest expectation of the creation eagerly waits for the revealing of the sons of God. For the creation was subjected to futility, not willingly, but because of Him who subjected it in hope; because the creation itself also will be delivered from the bondage of corruption into the glorious liberty of the children of God. For we know that the whole creation groans and labors*

with birth pangs together until now. Not only that, but we also who have the firstfruits of the Spirit, even we ourselves groan within ourselves, eagerly waiting for the adoption, the redemption of our body. For we were saved in this hope, but hope that is seen is not hope; for why does one still hope for what he sees? But if we hope for what we do not see, we eagerly wait for it with perseverance.

Likewise the Spirit also helps in our weaknesses. For we do not know what we should pray for as we ought, but the Spirit Himself makes intercession for us with groanings which cannot be uttered. (Romans 8:18–26)

The concept of groaning is mentioned three times in this passage. First, the groaning of creation. Creation was made to worship God and be in perfect divine order. But when man fell, creation fell. There are now earthquakes, hurricanes, tornadoes, and all kinds of ugly things. Creation groans because of the state that it's in. Second, humankind groans. We say, "Goodnight; things are bad. When is this going to end?" Third, the Holy Spirit groans. Isn't that something?

Do you need the Spirit's help in this time while you're waiting for the redemption of your body? When we turn on the news and see what's happening in the world, can we get help? Absolutely. The Holy Spirit helps us in these difficult times, and we need to lean heavily on Him. When we pray in the Spirit, He will intercede for us and help us in our weakness. If you never pray in the Spirit, you're just going to get weaker. Sometimes, I've been exhausted, and then I pray for 20 minutes in the Holy Ghost, and I think, *Who's tired? Not me!* It's amazing how the Spirit strengthens you.

When the world is falling apart, the antichrist spirit is everywhere, people are backsliding and acting like the Bible isn't real, and Christians are being persecuted all around the world, we can lean on and pray in the Holy Spirit.

> *Now He who searches the hearts knows what the mind of the Spirit is, because He makes intercession for the saints according to the will of God. And we know that all things work together for good to those who love God, to those who are the called according to His purpose.* (Romans 8:27–28)

The Lord will cause all things to work together for good because He knows your heart better than you know it, He knows the will of God, and He knows the mind of the Spirit for your day, your moment, and your occasion. Let the Holy Ghost pray through you, giving you miracles on the inside, miracles on the outside, and making all things work together for good in your life!

Have things become so desperate that you feel the devil is doing battle in your heart? Do you want to be saved from this attack and be redeemed for a life of eternal fellowship with a savior who is gentle, loving, and perfect? Then pray with me today:

> Lord, I repent of the sin in my life — of the years I rebelled against you and the times I rejected you. I accept Christ's sacrifice and ask Him to come into my heart to rule and reign over my life. I ask you to redeem me, restore me, and prepare me for eternity. I ask for the gift of discernment and for the refreshment of the Holy Spirit to fill my life and give me wisdom, strength, and work all things for my good. Thank you for all of these wonderful gifts. I pray all of this in Jesus's name, amen.

If you just prayed this prayer, you now have the victory over anything that may come against you!

No matter what circumstances you are faced with, no matter how the devil may try to attack you, no matter what is going on around you in the world — you already have the victory through the shed blood of Jesus and the power of the Holy Spirit.

It's not over until you win!

End Notes

Winning Through Deliverance

Page 2: *Jehovah:* "self-existent or Eternal." James Strong, *The New Strong's Complete Dictionary of Bible Words.* Nashville: Thomas Nelson Publishers (1996). s.v. "Jehovah."

Page 2: *El:* Strong, s.v. "el."

Page 2: *Hananiah:* Strong, s.v. "Hananiah."

Page 2: *Shadrach:* Mike and Victoria Campbell, "Shadrach." Updated May 29, 2020. Behind the Name. Accessed December 13, 2023, from https://www.behindthename.com/name/shadrach

Page 2: *Azariah:* Strong, s.v. "Azariah."

Page 2: *Abednego:* Mike and Victoria Campbell, "Abednego." Updated April 16, 2019. Behind the Name. Accessed December 13, 2023, from https://www.behindthename.com/name/abednego

Page 2: *Mishael:* Strong, s.v. "Mishael."

Page 2: *Belteshazzar:* Smith's Bible Dictionary, s.v. "Belteshazzar." Accessed December 13, 2023, from https://www.biblegateway.com/resources/smiths-bible-names-dictionary/Belteshazzar

Page 3: *Meshach:* "Meshach," Biblestudytools.com. Accessed December 13, 2023, from https://www.biblestudytools.com/dictionary/meshach/

Page 3: *Daniel:* Strong, s.v. "Daniel."

Winning Against the Devil

Page 51: *Strength:* Strong, s.v. "dunamis."

Page 57: *Commentary on Ecclesiastes 12:6:* Matthew Henry, *Commentary on the Whole Bible*, Grand Rapids: Zondervan Publishing House. 1972, page 809.

Winning Through Resurrection Power

Page 90: *Dunamis:* Strong, s.v. "dunamis."

Page 90: *Exousia:* Strong, s.v. "exousia."

Page 95: *Unleavened bread:* "Matzah," Wikipedia.org. Accessed December 14, 2023, from https://en.wikipedia.org/wiki/Unleavened_bread

Page 105: *Anastasis:* Strong, s.v. "anastasis."

Page 110: *An old hymn:* William P. Merrill, "Rise Up O Men of God," 1911. Accessed December 14, 2023, from https://hymnary.org/text/rise_up_o_men_of_god

Page 111: *Discern the Lord's body:* "διακρίνω," Thayer's Greek Lexicon. Accessed December 14, 2023, from https://www.blueletterbible.org/lexicon/g1252/kjv/tr/0-1/

Winning Against the Antichrist

Page 116: *Redeem:* Strong, s.v. "lutroo."

Page 119: *Regenerate:* Merriam-webster.com, s.v. "regenerate." Accessed December 14, 2023, from https://www.merriam-webster.com/dictionary/regenerate

Page 121: *Armageddon:* Strong, s.v. "Armageddon."

END NOTES

Page 123: *Megiddo:* Touristisrael.com. "Megiddo." Accessed December 14, 2023, from https://www.touristisrael.com/megiddo/9448/

Page 126: *Harpazo:* Biblestudytools.com, s.v. "harpazo." Accessed December 14, 2023, from https://www.biblestudytools.com/lexicons/greek/kjv/harpazo.html

Page 126: *Rapture:* Merriam-webster.com, s.v. "rapture." Accessed December 14, 2023, from https://www.merriam-webster.com/dictionary/rapture

Page 127: *Rapture and raptus*: Etymonline.com, s.v. "rapture (n.)." Accessed December 14, 2023, from https://www.etymonline.com/word/rapture

Page 127: *Atomos:* Strong, s.v. "atomos."

Page 130: *Rebuild the temple*: Got Questions Ministries. "Will there be an end times temple in Jerusalem?" Updated January 4, 2022. Accessed December 14, 2023, from https://www.gotquestions.org/end-times-temple.html

Page 132: *Diabolos:* Strong, s.v. "diabolos."

Page 136: *Assyrian empire*: National Geographic Society, "Assyrian Empire," updated October 19, 2023. Accessed December 14, 2023, from https://education.nationalgeographic.org/resource/assyrian-empire/

Page 151: *Jehoshaphat:* Strong, s.v. "Jehoshaphat."

Page 155: *Metanoeo:* Strong, s.v. "metanoeo."

Page 155: *Metamellomai:* Strong, s.v "metamellomai."

Page 179: *Commentary on James 4:10:* Matthew Henry, *Commentary on the Whole Bible*, page 1936.

About Marilyn

Encouraging, optimistic, always upbeat and energetic, even in her later years, Marilyn Hickey actively ministers internationally. As founder and president of *Marilyn & Sarah Ministries*, a non-profit ministry and humanitarian organization based in Denver, Colorado, Marilyn has traveled to over 140 countries and has impacted many nations around the world — from disaster relief efforts in Haiti, Indonesia, and Pakistan to providing food for the hungry in Mexico, Costa Rica, Russia, and the Philippines.

Her legacy includes significant ministry in Islamic countries. In 2016, over one million people attended her healing meeting in Karachi, Pakistan.

Marilyn has held audiences with government leaders and heads of state all over the world. She was the first woman to join the board of directors for Dr. David Yonggi

Cho (founder of the world's largest congregation, Yoido Full Gospel Church in South Korea).

Along with her daughter, Pastor Sarah Bowling, she co-hosts the daily television program, *Today with Marilyn & Sarah*, which is broadcast globally in nearly 200 countries with a potential viewing audience of over 2 billion households worldwide. Marilyn has also authored over 100 publications.

She and her late husband, Wallace, were married over 50 years and have two children and five grandchildren. Marilyn holds a Bachelor of Arts in Collective Foreign Languages from the University of Northern Colorado and an Honorary Doctor of Divinity from Oral Roberts University.

In 2015, Marilyn was honored at Oral Roberts University with the prestigious Lifetime Global Achievement Award. This award recognizes individuals, or organizations, that have made a significant impact in the history of ORU and around the world. In 2019, Marilyn also received an International Lifetime Peace Award from the Grand Imam and President of Pakistan.

In 2021, Marilyn was honored with two awards from the Assemblies of God Theological Seminary: The Pillar of Faith Award in acknowledgment of her worldwide impact on the church through biblical teaching and sustainable healing ministry; and the Smith Wigglesworth Award, given on behalf of the entire Assemblies of God fellowship in acknowledgment of her decades of service worldwide.

Marilyn's greatest passion and desire is to continue being a bridge-builder in countries around the world, and she shows no signs of stopping.

Receive Jesus Christ as Lord and Savior of Your Life

You can have Jesus's joy, peace, protection, and provision in your life starting today. You can also know for sure that you will have life after death in heaven.

God sent Jesus Christ to be the Savior of the world. First Timothy 2:5–6 says, *"For there is one God and one Mediator between God and men, the Man Christ Jesus, who gave Himself a ransom for all, to be testified in due time."*

The Bible tells us how we can receive Jesus as Savior:

> *If you confess with your mouth the Lord Jesus and believe in your heart that God has raised Him from the dead, you will be saved. For with the heart one believes unto righteousness, and with the mouth confession is made unto salvation.*
> (Romans 10:9–10)

Would you like to begin a personal relationship with God and Jesus right now? You can! Simply pray this prayer in sincerity:

Heavenly Father, I acknowledge that I need your help. I am not able to change my life or circumstances through my own efforts. I know that I have made some wrong decisions in my life, and at this moment I turn away from those ways of thinking and acting. I believe you have provided a way for me through Jesus to receive your blessings and help in my life. Right now, I believe and confess Jesus as my Lord and Savior. I ask Jesus to come into my heart and give me a new life, by your Spirit. I thank you for saving me, and I ask for your grace and mercy in my life. I pray this in Jesus's name. Amen.

If you just prayed to make Jesus your Lord, we want to know!

Please call us today — toll free — at 888-637-4545.

We will pray for you and send you a special gift to help you in your new life with Christ.

Learn more about Marilyn & Sarah Ministries

Marilyn & Sarah Ministries: marilynandsarah.org
Check out our free downloads that include Bible reading plans, teaching notes, inspirational graphics, spiritual self-assessments, and lists of verses based on topic.

Online Master Classes: mentoredbymarilyn.org
Marilyn is passing her mantle on to you! Through her anointed master classes, you will be mentored in strategic areas that will take you to the next level of victory and fulfillment in your life and ministry. This is an incredible opportunity to mentored by Marilyn!

Connect with Marilyn:

- MarilynHickeyMinistries
- MarilynandSarah
- MarilynHickeyMinistries
- MarilynHickeyMinistries